法務英語入門−改訂第Ⅱ版

法務英語入門 – 改訂第Ⅱ版

後藤 浩司 著

信山社サイテック

はじめに

　本書の初版を上梓してから7年が経とうとしている。いま改訂版の発行に当たり，初版および増補2版のはしがきを辿りながら少し述べてみたいと思う。
　翻ってみると，初版の発行から現在までの間に世の中はずいぶんと変化してきた。英語もその例外ではない。殊に，バブル経済の崩壊後，多くの外資系企業が進出し，日本企業への資本参加・提携や吸収・合併が盛んに行われるようになってきた。そうなるとトップの役員だけでなく，上司となる社員や同僚も送り込まれてくることになり，会議だけでなく普段のコミュニケーションも英語が必要になってくる。このように，この数年の間に英語を取り巻く環境が大きく変貌し，結果として国際化が現実のものとなったといえるだろう。
　ただ，外資系といえども日本国内で事業するのだから，日本の法律に準拠しなければならないのは当然のことであるが，わが国のビジネス形態が変わっていくのは間違いないことだろう。それを受けてのことかどうかは定かではないが，平成12年12月28日に特許庁はビジネスモデル特許の審査基準を発表した。殊に，情報産業などの先端分野での特許競争は激しく，わが国も様々な分野においてグローバル・スタンダードが求められる時代となってきた証左といえよう。
　なお，この特許に関してだが，米国特許法では特許の対象がuseful artであり，それを「有用な技術」と訳すことが通例となっている。ところが日本の特許法では，特許の対象である発明は「自然法則を利用した技術的思想の創作で高度なもの。」と言うことになっていて，特許の対象を技術と切り離して考えることができないでいる。それで，米国特許法のuseful artを「有用な技術」，prior artを「先行技術」と一般的に訳してきたわけである。ところが，ビジネスモデル特許などが論ぜられる時代になると，art＝技術という翻訳が成り立たなくなるような気がする。そこで，artを「技能」と訳すべきではないかと考えている。
　さらに振り返って考えると，日本では「意匠」が特許法とは独立した意匠法によって保護されているが，米国では特許法で保護している。そこで，米国特許法のuseful artを「有用な技術」と訳したのでは，「意匠」を含ませることにはならず，

v

はじめに

「art＝技術」は無理な訳語になってしまう。

　また，初版のはしがきの中で，二重否定＝肯定と単純に考えてはならないことや，長いセンテンスからなる英文の訳し方に数学の「代入法」を利用することなどについて触れたが，この二重否定＝肯定が必ずしも成立しないという具体例などについては，本書で新たに節を設けて説明する。そして，長いセンテンスからなる英文の訳し方の具体例についても特許関係のところで紹介する。

　次に，米国企業の法務部門の組織と活動について，新たに章を設けて紹介する。一般的に，米国では特許部は会社の法務部門に属していることが多いので，特許関係のことを少し本書に加えることにした。ただ，ここでは最も一般的な特許に関する技術対象を選んだ。それは，日本の技術をベースとする Magnetic Soroban（マグネチックソロバン）と言う名称の米国特許である。なお，そのベースとなった日本語の資料や助言等に関して，元弁理士会会長の田中武文先生に大変お世話になった。

　ところで，英語の変遷についてもう少し触れてみる。言葉は生き物であり，時代と共に常に変化しているのだから，文法は法律のように強制力があるわけではない。大部分の人たちが認めて使っている慣用例（usage）のことであろう。したがって，英文法に対しても柔軟な考え方を持つことが許されるはずである。例えば，筆者が"The Law of Chemical, Metallurgical and Pharmaceutical Patents"の本を訳していたときである。この本の104頁，12～13行に米国特許法第102条(a)に関する以下の記載があった。

　　　"Furthermore, in order to anticipate, the prior knowledge and use must be accesible to the public."

　　　（逐語訳すると"さらに，先行物件としての要件を満たすために，先知および先使用は公衆の使用しうる状態になければならない"）

　すなわち，"新規制を喪失させるためには，先に知られていることや，先に使用されていることが公然のものでなければならない"となる。

　"anticipate"は，他動詞で目的語が必要である。しかし，上述の引例文にはanticipateの目的語がなく，自動詞として使用されている。上述の書物はその方面の専門書であり，しかも20数名の専門家が編集に参加している。したがって，特許に関する英語の慣用では，当業者の間でanticipateが自動詞としても使用されるようになったと理解される。なおその後，米連邦最高裁の判決中でも同様な使用例を見た

はじめに

ことがあるが，残念ながらそれがどの判決にあったのか思い出せないでいる。
　さらに，英文法を必ずしも絶対視べきでない趣旨の言葉を以下に引用する。
　　　　"……may not be the slave of the grammar……
　　　In construction of statutes and presumably also in construction of federal rules…
　　　…, but context in which word appears must be controlling factor.（Black Law Dictionary, 979頁右欄)"
　　　（……文法の奴隷になってはならない。……
　　　　制定法の解釈，またたぶん連邦規則の解釈の際にも，……
　　　　言葉が出ている前後関係が支配的要素でなければならない。)
　上述の引用文は，文を正しく解釈するには文法の理屈よりも文脈，すなわち，文の前後関係が大切なことを教えている。
　最後に，本書が3版を重ねることになったのは著者の望外の喜びであり，この出版に当たり信山社サイテックの四戸孝治氏にはいろいろとお世話になった。ここに，改めて感謝の意を表す。

平成13年1月
著者　後　藤　浩　司

目　次

法務英語入門 – 改訂第Ⅱ版

第1章　法務英語 ― 基礎の基礎 …………………………………… 1

　これが分かれば国際業務が分かる（1）
　　a）shall と may（1）
　　b）二重否定＝肯定は必ずしも正しくない（2）
　　c）subject と object（3）

第2章　米国会社の法務部門 …………………………………………… 5

　第1節　法務部門（Legal Division）の組織と活動（5）
　　a）法務部（Legal Department）（6）
　　b）秘書部（The Secretary's Department）（11）
　　c）特許部（Patent Department）（20）
　　d）税務部（Tax Department）（28）
　　e）保険部（Insurance Department）（32）
　　f）法務部門の究極の目的 ― 再び上席副社長の言葉（39）
　第2章　特許と英語（41）
　　a）特許関係の英語（41）
　　　（1）特許の英語（41）
　　　（2）特許制度（41）
　　　（3）明　細　書（41）
　　　（4）明細書の翻訳（42）
　　b）特許明細書（42）
　　　（1）超ミニ米国特許明細書（英文和訳）（42）
　　　（2）算盤に関する特許（和文英訳と英文和訳）（48）
　　c）特許の文法と長いセンテンスの英訳法（59）

　　　　　　(1) 化学特許明細書における動詞のテンス（*59*）
　　　　　　(2) 法律の条文，特許のクレームなど（*69*）
　　　d）その　他（*78*）
　　　　　　(1) 特許を受ける権利の譲渡書（*78*）
　　　　　　(2) 特許譲渡に関する法的根拠（*79*）
　　　　　　(3) 基本的な図面に関する用語（*84*）

第 3 章　特約店・代理店契約 ……………………………………… *87*

　　第 1 節　特約店契約（*88*）
　　第 2 節　代理店契約（*99*）
　　第 3 節　売買契約（*108*）

第 4 章　会社の定款 ……………………………………………… *135*

　　第 1 節　米国会社の定款（*136*）
　　第 2 節　米国会社の決議書（*151*）
　　第 3 節　米国会社の目的の翻訳（*157*）
　　第 4 節　日本の株式会社の定款（*167*）

第 5 章　法務関係における米国の教育 ………………………… *187*

　　第 1 節　Public Administration 関係のスクール
　　　　　　― 官庁関係の文章作成 ―（*188*）
　　　　a）演習趣旨（*189*）
　　　　b）課　題（*190*）
　　　　c）作成要領（*192*）
　　　　d）作成準備で注意すること（*194*）
　　第 2 節　speech と drama の英語訓練
　　　　　　― 日本人ビジネスマンにも参考になる ―（*196*）
　　　　a）教材 1（the の発音）（*196*）
　　　　b）教材 2（t の発音）（*198*）
　　　　c）教材 3（英文のリズム）（*200*）

第1章　法務英語 ─ 基礎の基礎

これが分かれば国際業務が分かる

　ここで紹介する語句はあまりにも当然過ぎる基礎であって，つい見逃してしまいがちであるが，頻繁に使われていながら大変重要な語句でもある。特に，この使い方を間違えると全く解釈に違いが生じてしまうことになる。そこで，代表的な例をあげて解説する。

a）shall と may

　法務関係の英訳をするときには，「法律のshall」，［法律may］などと称して，特に注意を払う語句である。前者は「〜するものとする」，後者は「〜をすることができる」を意味する。
　この具体例として，以下に刑法第43条を示す。

【例　文】
（未遂減免）
第43条　犯罪の実行に着手してこれを遂げなかった者は，その刑を軽減することができる。ただし，自己の意志により犯罪を中止したときは，その刑を減軽し，または免除する。

【訳　文】
Article 43. (Criminal Attempt: Non-completed Crimes)
　The punishment of a person who has begun but not completed the commission of a crime may be reduced. However, if he has stopped the criminal acts voluntarily in the course of its commission, the punishment shall be reduced remitted.

第1章　法務英語 ― 基礎の基礎

　以前，筆者が米軍に勤務していた頃，法務将校は日本刑法の英訳文を，筆者は六法全書の刑法を見ながら会議をしていた。ところが，次第に話が噛み合わなくなってきた。なぜなのかと思いながら将校の見ていた英訳刑法文を覗いたところ，その第43条の「〜できる」と「〜する」の部分が共に，英文では「shall」となっていた。要するに，「shall」と「may」が峻別して使われていなかったことが判明した。

　この解釈は，障碍未遂の場合には，刑を軽減するかどうかは自由裁量の問題であり，中止未遂の場合には，刑を必ず減刑するか免除しなければならないことになっている。英訳では法的効果が不明確になってしまっている。その後，法務省から但し訳が発表されたのが上記の英訳である。

b）二重否定＝肯定は必ずしも正しくない

　これも上述の例と同じように，「日本国における国際連合の軍隊の地位に関する協定の実施に伴う刑事特別法」の関係で日本刑法の勉強をする必要が生じ，そのための会議の際であった。やはり解釈に違いが出て話が噛み合わなくなってきた。

　その問題とは，刑法19条第2項の「没収は，犯人以外の者に属しない物に限り，これをすることができる」の解釈であった。すなわち，事件に関連した物は，筆者は「没収可能である」と主張し，法務省でも同様だと言ったのだが，その将校はあまり納得していないようだった。そこで，英訳文を見ると以下のように記載されていた。

Confiscation may be made only in cases where the object to be confiscated belongs to the criminal.

　この英訳では，「没収すべき物が犯人に属する場合のみ没収できる」となってしまい，意味が違ってしまうことになる。ただし，この英訳はある有名な出版社から出された本である。

　刑法第19条第2項の趣旨は，そのものが犯人に属する場合および無主物，例えば海岸の漂流物，路傍の石ころのようなものは没収できることになっている。ところが，上述の英訳では，無主物のようなものは没収できないことになってしまう。すなわち，没収すべき物が犯人に属する場合だけに限定されてしまうことになる。これは，二重否定＝肯定と単純に考えて訳したためであろう。

そこで，原文の趣旨を正しく伝えている法務省での翻訳を以下に示す。

A thing may be confiscated only if it doest not belong to a person other than the criminal.

c) subject と object

筆者が若い頃に翻訳の仕事をしていたときのことである。ある米国人の検閲者(reviewer)から，日本人はsubjectとobjectを混合して使っていると指摘されたことがある。ただその時は，翻訳する者にとっては当然理解していると自負していたので，「変なことを言うな」と思っていた。しかし，ネイティブの学識者から指摘されると，どうも気になってきた。そこで，いろいろ文献を見たり英英辞典を調べていくうちに，どうも「subject＝主題，課題，object＝対象，目的」だけではないと気がついたのであった。すなわち，ケースバイケースで使い分けるのであって，subjectを「対象」と訳した方が理解しやすいことや，同じ「主題」でもobjectを使ったりすることを学んだのだった。このようにして，subjectとobjectの微妙な相違を会得することができた。ただ，この相違を説明する例文が法律文書には少なく苦労していたのだが，ようやく見つけることができたので，これらの相違を示す例文を以下に紹介する。

・例―1
　米特許法102条　"the subject matter sought to be patented"［特許を請求した発明の主題(subject matter)］，これを「特許を取得しようとする対象」とすると理解しやすい。

・例―2
　パリ条約第4条C-(4)　"A subsequent application for the same subject as a previous first application"［最初の出願と同一の対象について … 後の出願］；同条約第4条の3　"the use of … forming the subject of the patent … in the … of aircraft or land vehicles"［航空機または車両 … に関する特許権の対象である … を使用すること］

第2章　米国会社の法務部門

第1節　法務部門(Legal Division)の組織と活動

　その法務部門は六つある会社のスタッフ部門で最も小さく，約100名の社員で構成されている。この法務部門は以下の五つの部から構成されている。
① 法務部（Legal Department）
② 秘書部（Secretary's Department）
③ 特許部（Patent Department）
④ 税務部（Tax Department）
⑤ 保険部（Insurance Department）
　以下，英文の資料により米社法務部門の組織とその活動について述べる。
　上述の「部」を構成する法務部門の指揮をとるJ．A氏（弁護士）は，取締役会のメンバーであるとともに上席副社長である。前職の略歴は，税務裁判所のスタッフを経てワシントンにあるローファームの元パートナーである。その法務部門について，同上席副社長は次のように述べている。

【例　文】

　"It's a service organization," "It doesn't make anything; it doesn't sell anything; it doesn't produce anything. It simply renders service."
　Because of the broad diversity of work handled by the division, JA says that he delegates responsibility extensively. "It's a physical impossibility to keep track of everything that goes on in the division. Much of it is specialized, and I rely on the judgment of my staff to work directly with those concerned and to call my attention to situations which I need to know about. "While he assumes ultimate responsibility for legal decisions of the group, he has confidence in the ability and integrity of those working with him."

第2章　米国会社の法務部門

【語句の説明】

Because of the broad diversity of work：業務の広汎にして多様性に富んでいるために
delegates responsibility extensively：権限を広範囲にわたり委譲している
a physical impossibility：物理的に不可能
keep track of everything：一切の業務を絶えず注意する
rely on the judgment of my staff：スタッフの判断に任せる
work directly with those concerned：関与している人たちと直接仕事をする
call my attention：私の注意を促す
assumes ultimate responsibility：最終責任を負う
 for legal decisions of the group：部門の法的判断については
the ability and integrity：能力と誠実性

> 【訳　文】
>
> 　それ（法務部門）はサービス組織であり，何もつくらず，何も販売せず，何も製造しない，単にサービスを提供するだけである。
> 　法務部門で行われている一切の業務を絶えず注意することは，物理的に不可能である。その多くは専門化されており，関与している人たちと直接仕事をし，かつ私が知る必要がある状況について，注意を促すように要求することをスタッフの判断に任せている。同部門の法的判断の最終責任は自分が負うが，ここで働いている者の能力と誠実性に信頼をおいている。

　同法務部門の扱う業務の広汎にして多様性に富んでいるために，同上席副社長は，その権限を広範囲にわたり委譲していると述べている。

a）法　務　部（**Legal Department**）

> 【例　文】
>
> 　The smallest of the five departments in the Legal Division is the Legal Department with two attorneys and their secretaries. Many companies turn to outside counsel for help with legal problems. While ABC does use some outside legal counsel, it minimizes such assistance. "For one thing" it takes a tremendous amount of time to educate outside counsel in the details of our

> business. Through constant saturation in the technical and business aspects of company operations, members of the Legal Department staff have an advantage.

【語句の説明】

two attorneys and their secretaries：2名の弁護士とその秘書達

outside counsel：外部の弁護士

minimizes：最小限にする

a tremendous amount of time：途方もない時間量

educate outside counsel in the details of our business：わが社の業務の詳細について外部弁護士を教育する

through constant saturation：絶え間なく充分にさらす

the technical and business aspects of company operations：会社業務の技術面ならびにビジネス面

an advantage：優位な立場，優位点

---【訳　文】---
> 　法務部は部門内部の五つの部の中で最も小さい部である。その構成は2名の弁護士とその秘書達である。米国でも法律問題に関して外部の弁護士に依頼する会社が多いが，ABCではある程度外部弁護士を利用するが，このようなことは最小限にしている。「一つには，わが社の業務の詳細について，外部弁護士を教育するのには途方もない時間を必要とする。絶え間なく会社業務の技術面ならびにビジネス面に充分さらされることにより，法務部のメンバーは優位な立場にある。」

---【例　文】---
> 　Most of F's contacts are with the various marketing or sales departments of the company. In this area there are many questions on the interpretation of antitrust laws, and restraint of trade. "Our sales representatives may ask," F explains, "whether we can legally meet a lower price offered by competitors, whether particular products can be merchandised through distributors, whether price differentials can be based on quantities ordered. We have to give an opinion, and recommend a course of action."

第2章　米国会社の法務部門

【語句の説明】

the various marketing or sales departments：色々のマーケットあるいは販売部門
the interpretation of antitrust laws：独禁法の解釈
restraint of trade：競業の抑制
sales representatives：販売員
whether we can legally meet a lower price offered by competitors：競業者が提供するより安い価格に，法的に対応することができるかどうか
whether particular products can be merchandised through distributors：特定の商品を販売業者を通じて商品化することができるかどうか
price differentials：価格上の差異
can be based on quantities ordered：注文を受けた量を根拠とすることができるかどうか
a course of action：とるべき行動

【訳　文】

　F弁護士が担当する業務の大部分は会社の色々のマーケットあるいは販売部門に関係している。この領域には独禁法の解釈および競業の抑制に関し多くの問題がある。「わが社の販売員が，われわれは競業者が提供するより安い価格に法的に対応することができるかどうか，特定の商品を販売業者を通じて商品化することができるかどうか，価格上の差異は注文を受けた量を根拠とすることができるかどうか，わが部は意見を出し，いかなる行動をとるべきかについてアドバイスしなければならない。

【例　文】

　Recommendations are not easy. The law today may be different from the law tomorrow, and the Legal Department has to be prepared to offer its opinion on what the law is today while keeping a careful watch on current judicial decisions which may change that law tomorrow.

【語句の説明】

a careful watch：注意深い見守り
on current judicial decisions：現行の司法による判決について

第 1 節　法務部門 (Legal Division) の組織と活動

may change that law tomorrow：その法律は明日変更するかも知れない

---【訳　文】---

　アドバイスすることは容易なことではない。今日の法律は明日の法律と異なるかもしれない。また法務部は，現行の司法による判決－その法律は明日変更するかも知れない－を注意深く見守りながら，いまの法律がどのようなものであるかについて意見を出す用意ができていなくてはならない。

---【例　文】---

　F also specializes in acquisitions. During the past year he has become almost a regular commuter to Mexico to assist in particular problems there, and he has spent some time in Australia. He finds his job difficult, challenging, and exciting. "I don't do much trial work," he says, "but all other aspects of law are here. It's something like being an attorney in a city of 1 3.000 people, with all the problems which would be encountered."

【語句の説明】

specializes in acquisitions：吸収合併を専門とする；普通の合併なら merger
almost a regular commuter to ～：～へのほとんど定期的な通勤者
difficult, challenging, and exciting：困難だがやりがいがあり，エキサイティングな
trial work：訴訟の仕事
something like being an attorney in a city of 1 3.000 people：人口13,000人の市で弁護士をやっているようなもの〈会社の従業員数が概ね1,300名であることを考慮している〉。
all the problems which would be encountered：遭遇するであろうあらゆる問題

---【訳　文】---

　同弁護士は，また吸収合併を専門としている。前年中，彼はほとんどメキシコへの定期的な通勤者になってしまった。その目的はそこで特別重要な問題の手伝いをするためであった。また，オーストラリアでもかなりの時間を過ごした。彼は，自分の仕事な困難だがやりがいがあり，エキサイティングなものであると認識している。そのことを，自身の言葉で次のように言っている。

第2章　米国会社の法務部門

「私は訴訟の仕事はあまりやらない。しかし，ここではそのほかのすべての法務業務を行っている。それは，人口13,000人の市で弁護士をやっているようなものであり，そこで遭遇するであろうあらゆる問題が含まれている。」

【例　文】

H also provides legal counsel on marketing problem and reviews much of the company's advertising, technical literature, and publicity releases to be certain that statements and claims are valid and within the requirements of the law. He provides legal counsel to the Purchasing Department in its complicated problems which can become as tangled as marketing questions. Real estate transactions of the company require attention, and H carries this portfolio for the parent company and subsidiaries.

【語句の説明】

provides legal counsel on marketing problem：マーケット関係の法律問題の相談業務を行う

reviews much of ～：～の多くについて検討する

the company's advertising, technical literature, and publicity releases：会社の広告，技術文献，発表文書

to be certain that ～：～を確認するために

statements and claims are valid：記載内容や主張が正当である

within the requirements of the law：法律要件にかなう

to the Purchasing Department：購買部に

complicated problems：複雑な問題

as tangled as marketing questions：マーケット関係の問題として紛糾する可能性のある

real estate transactions：不動産関係の取引

require attention注意を要する

H carries this portfolio：H弁護士はこの業務を行う

for the parent company and subsidiaries：親会社と小会社のために

10

第1節　法務部門(Legal Division)の組織と活動

---【訳　文】---

　もう一人の弁護士のH氏は，マーケット関係の法律問題の相談に応ずるとともに会社の広告，技術文献，発表文書の多くについて，その記載内容や主張が正当であるか法律要件にかなうか否かを確認するために検討する。また，同氏はマーケット関係の問題として紛糾する可能性のある複雑な問題について，購買部に法律上の助言を与える。会社の不動産関係の取引は注意を要するので，H弁護士はその関係業務を親会社と小会社のためにも行っている。

---

b）秘　書　部（The Secretary's Department）

---【例　文】---

　Anyone who has ever joined a PTA or a neighborhood flower club knows that the secretary is the one who keeps the minutes of meetings and writes the letters. These are also included in the responsibilities of a corporate secretary, and while he doesn't have to take care of all correspondence he has a few more responsibilities, spelled out not only by the articles of incorporation but by legal decisions and precedents. Not surprisingly, then, the secretary is generally a lawyer, and ABC Company is no exception to this generality.

【語句の説明】
a neighborhood flower club：町内のフラワークラブ
keep the minutes of meetings：会議の議事録を保管する
the responsibilities of a corporate secretary：会社秘書役の責務
spelled out by the articles of incorporation：定款に定められている
legal decisions and precedents：裁判所の判決，判例
no exception to this generality：この一般性に対して例外でない

---【訳　文】---

　PTAや町内のフラワークラブに参加したことのある人なら誰でも，秘書が会議の議事録を保管し，手紙を書く人であることを知っている。これらの仕事がまた会社秘書役の責務に含まれ，さらに必ずしも全部の通信文を取り扱わなくてもよいが，その他に定款や裁判所の判決や判例を詳しく説明する責任を有す

第2章 米国会社の法務部門

る。驚くべきことではないが，秘書は一般的に弁護士であり，わが社もこの一般性に対して例外ではない。

【例　文】

　In addition to being a custodian of the legal records ("Records are the foot-prints of the corporation," FR says, "the proof of the existence and of the actions of the corporation as a legal person.") the secretary is responsible for the orderly handling of stockholder relations in accordance with regulations of the Securities and Exchange Commission and the New York Stock Exchange. His office handles registration and transfer of stock and proxy statements and is responsible for compliance with legal requirements governing the calling of and the conduct of meetings of stockholders, directors, and the executive committee and for reporting on them. F also serves as secretary for all the domestic subsidiaries of ABC.

　But FR has many responsibilities other than those of a corporate secretary. He has become the company's expert in providing a legal basis for the use of ABC Company products in a number of fields where their introduction and use is controlled by municipal, state, or federal laws.

【語句の説明】

In addition to～：～であるほかに
being a custodian of the legal records：法的記録文書の管理人
records are the foot-prints of the corporation：記録文書は会社の足跡である
the proof of the existence and of the actions of the corporation：会社の存在と活
　動に関する証明
as a legal person：法人として
responsible for the orderly handling：適正に取り扱う責任を有する
stockholder relations：株主関係
in accordance with regulations of～：～の規則にしたがって
the Securities and Exchange Commission：有価証券市場委員会
the New York Stock Exchange：ニューヨーク市場

第1節　法務部門（Legal Division）の組織と活動

registration and transfer of stock and proxy statements：株式の登録および移転ならびに代理人関係の書類
responsible for compliance with legal requirements：法的要件にしたがうようにする責任を有する
governing the calling of and the conduct of meetings of：会議の招集ならびに運営
the executive committee：執行委員
for reporting on them：それらの事項を報告する
all the domestic subsidiaries of ABC：ABC社の国内に存在するすべての子会社
providing a legal basis for the use of ～：～の使用について法的根拠を与える

―【訳　文】――――――――――――――――――――――

　F弁護士によると，秘書は法的記録文書の管理人であるほかに，自身の言葉で次の如く述べている。「記録文書は，会社の足跡，すなわち，法人としての会社の存在と行動に関する証明である。」
　有価証券市場委員会およびニューヨーク市場の規則にしたがって株主関係を適正に取り扱う責任を有し，彼の事務所では株式の登録および移転ならびに代理人関係の書類を扱い，株主，取締役，執行委員に係る会議の招集ならびに運営を定めている法的要件にしたがうように努め，かつそれらの事項を報告する責任を有する。また同弁護士はABC社の国内に存在するすべての子会社の秘書役もつとめている。
　また，同弁護士は会社の秘書役としての職務のほかに，多くの責任を有している。ABC社の製品の紹介と用途に関しては市，州，連邦法の支配を受けている多くの分野におけるそれらの製品の使用について法的根拠を与える専門家となっている。

―【例　文】――――――――――――――――――――――

　"It is a basic fact of selling," says F, "that Government regulations defines the market for many of today's products. In building application, for example, building codes control the use of materials such as our XYZ acrylic plastic for exterior panels, glazing, sky-lights, lighting diffusers, or interior partitions. In the pharmaceutical field, no human or animal drug can be sold without first complying with many state and federal regulations."

第2章　米国会社の法務部門

【語句の説明】

a basic fact of selling：販売の基本的事実
Government regulations defines ～：政府の規則が～を限定している
market for many of today's products：多くの今日の製品のための市場
in building application：建築工事への応用
building codes control the use of materials：建築法規が使用を統制している
our XYZ acrylic plastic for：わが社のアクリル系プラスチックXYZ
exterior panels：外部パネル
glazing：ガラス工事
sky-lights：スカイライト
lighting diffusers：照明拡散具
interior partitions：インテリアパーテーション
in the pharmaceutical field：薬剤の分野では
human or animal drug：医薬品あるいは動物用薬剤
without complying with many state and federal regulations：州や連邦の多くの法規にしたがわなくては

【訳　文】

　同弁護士は次のように言っている。「政府の規則が，多くの今日の製品のために市場を限定していることは，販売の基本的事実である。」たとえば，建築工事への応用に当たり，外部パネル，ガラス工事，天窓，照明拡散具，あるいはインテリアパーテーション用のわが社のアクリル系プラスチックXYZ資材の使用を建築法規が統制している。薬剤の分野では，医薬品あるいは動物用薬剤は，先ず州や連邦の多くの法規にしたがわなくては販売することができない。

この資料は若干古いものであるが，現在ならシックハウス防止のために注意しなくてはならないであろう。

【例　文】

　When he was hired, F says, Mr. ABC assigned him primary responsibility for the company's compliance with public laws governing the safe use of company materials. "Mr. ABC wanted to be sure that we knew our legal responsibilities and that we met them in advance of our entry into any field of market

第1節　法務部門(Legal Division)の組織と活動

development." He and his staff are still at that job. It is a double-edged responsibility. On the one hand, there has to be assurance that ABC is not recommending products for applications for which they are not suited. On the other hand, there is the necessity for assuring that government regulations do not inhibit unnecessarily the use of ABC products in appropriate applications.

【語句の説明】
when he was hired：彼が採用されたときに
primary responsibility：主な責務
the company's compliance with public laws：会社が公法を守るようにすること
governing the safe use of company materials：会社資材の安全使用を統制している
wanted to be sure that：間違いなくするべく望んでいたのは～である
we knew our legal responsibilities：われわれが法的責任を知る
we meet them in advance：われわれは予めそれを守る
our entry into any field of market development：市場開発の分野に参入する
he and his staff are still at that job：同弁護士と彼のスタッフは現在でも同じ仕事を行っている
a double-edged responsibility：両刃の剣ような責任
not recommending products for applications：用途に製品を勧めない
do not inhibit unnecessarily the use of ABC products：わが社の製品の使用を不当に制限しない
in appropriate applications：適正な用途での使用

【訳　文】
　F弁護士によると，同弁護士が入社したときに，ABC社長から与えられた主な責務は，会社資材の安全使用を統制している公法を会社が守るようにすることであった。社長が間違いなくするべく望んでいたのは，われわれが法的責任を知り，かつ市場開発の分野に参入する前に予めその責任の遵守を確保するすることであった。同弁護士と彼のスタッフは現在でも同じ仕事を行っている。それは両刃の剣のような責任である。一方においては，会社が不適切な用途の使用に製品を勧めないことであり，他方において政府の規則がわが社の製品の

第2章　米国会社の法務部門

適正な用途での使用を不当に制限しないようにする必要性があるからである。

　F弁護士は入社してから数十年，同じ分野の仕事をしていることから見ると，この会社は終身雇用制を採用している。

---【例　文】---

　F points out that until 1955 no building codes provided for the use of plastics. If the use of a plastic was not provided for under a building code, it could not be used. In the 12 years since then, many codes have been rewritten and R's group has been involved in much of the legal work which has opened sizable markets for XYZ and other ABC products. The legal work, incidentally, has been accompanied by the development of test methods and the design of standards.

【語句の説明】
building codes：建築法規
provided for the use of plastics：プラスチックの使用を規定した
if the use of a plastic was not provided for：プラスチックの使用が建築法規に規定されていない場合には
has been involved in much of the legal work：法務業務の多くに参加した
has opened sizable markets for ～：～のために大きな市場が開いた
incidentally：偶然にも
development of test methods：試験方法の開発
the design of standards：基準の立案

---【訳　文】---

　F弁護士が指摘しているのは，1955年までは建築法規にはプラスチックの使用に関する規定が存在しなかったことである。プラスチックの使用が建築法規に規定されていない場合には，使用することができなかった。それから12年経って多くの規則が改正され，Rのグループは，XYZやその他のわが社の製品のために大きな市場が開かれたことにより法務業務の多くに巻き込まれてしまった。偶然なことであるが，その法務業務には試験方法の開発と基準の立案が伴った。

第 1 節　法務部門（Legal Division）の組織と活動

【例　文】

　AI's particular area of responsibility is building codes and regulations concerning the use of ABC products. Most of his work involves laws and regulations which affect the sale of XYZ.

　Building codes are the rules that require structures to be fire safe and structurally safe. They represent an effort to keep fire hazards within reasonable limits.

【語句の説明】

particular area of responsibility：責任を負う特別の分野

building codes and regulations concerning the use of ABC products：ABC社製品の使用に関する建築法規

affect the sale of XYZ：XYZの販売に影響を与える

require structures to be fire safe and structurally safe：耐火性を有しかつ構造的に安全であるということを要求する

represent an effort：努力を示す

keep fire hazards within reasonable limits：火災による危険を合理的限度内にとどめる

【訳　文】

　AI弁護士が責任を負う特別の分野としては，ABC社製品の使用に関する建築法規である。彼の仕事の大部分は，XYZの販売に影響を与える法規に関係している。

　建築法規は，構造物が耐火性を有しかつ構造的に安全であるということを要求する法規である。建築法規は火災による危険を合理的限度内にとどめようとする努力を示している。

【例　文】

　Increasingly sophisticated building materials and increasingly sophisticated building methods do not eliminate the necessity for keeping an eye on the safety of building construction. In general, this function has been assigned to the building officials of cities and municipalities, but many small cities do not have

17

第 2 章　米国会社の法務部門

> the facilities for developing their own codes. As a consequence, large regional building code groups have evolved, each of which attempts to write model codes for its area. These model codes are then made available to the municipalities and may be adopted in whole or in part.

【語句の説明】

increasingly sophisticated building materials（methods）：ますます高度化する建築資材（方法）

do not eliminate the necessity for～：～する必要性が無くなることはない

keeping an eye on the safety of building construction：ビル建設の安全性を監視する

this function：この職務

has been assigned to the building officials：建築関係の担当官にまかせられていた

As a consequence：その結果（必然的な）

large regional building code groups have evolved：大きな地域的建築法規グループが関係した

attempts to write model codes for its area：その地域のためにモデル法規を作成しようと試みる

may be adopted in whole or in part：その全部あるいは一部が採用されるかもしれない

> 【訳　文】
>
> 　建築資材と建築方法がますます高度化しても，ビル建設の安全性を監視する必要性が無くなることはない。一般的に，この職務は市当局の建築関係の担当官にまかせられていた。しかし多くの小都市では，自らの法規を開発する施設を有していない。その結果，大きな地域的建築法規グループが関係し，そのグループの各々がその地域のためにモデル法規を作成しようと試みている。これらのモデル法規は市当局により利用可能とされ，さらにその全てあるいは一部が採用されるかもしれない。

第1節　法務部門(Legal Division)の組織と活動

【例　文】

　F.H works with the groups charged with writing codes. Through him, ABC is often called on for assistance in defining acceptable plastics and in drafting standards of good practice to govern the use of plastics in buildings. Much of this work requires large-scale testing to determine what the hazards may be and what techniques can be used effectively to control them. One special test facility has been constructed at the Philadelphia plant in which burning and combustion tests are conducted to determine the safety of materials and installation.

【語句の説明】

F.H works with the groups：F.H弁護士はグループに協力して仕事をする
charged with writing codes：法規の作成を任せられている
is often called on for assistance：しばしば協力を求められる
in defining acceptable plastics：容認できるプラスチックを限定する
in drafting standards of good practice：良好な慣例基準を作成する
govern the use of plastics in buildings：建物内でのプラスチックの使用を規制する
large-scale testing：大規模な試験
determine what the hazards may be：どんな危険が存在する可能性があるか
what techniques can be used effectively to control them：それを制御するためにどんな技術が有効に用いることができるか
one special test facility：一つの特別試験施設
burning and combustion tests：燃焼試験
determine the safety of materials and installation：資材の耐火性および備え付け方法を決定する

【訳　文】

　F.H弁護士は法規の作成を任せられているグループに協力して仕事をしている。わが社は彼を通じて、しばしば承認対象のプラスチックの定義を定め、あるいは建物内でのプラスチックの使用を規制する良好な慣例基準を作成するのに協力を求められる。これらの仕事の多くは、どんな危険が存在する可能性があるか、それを制御するためにどんな技術が有効に用いることができるかを決定するために大規模な試験を必要とする。一つの特別試験施設がフィラデル

フィア工場につくられた。その施設では資材の耐火性および備え付け方法を決定するために燃焼試験が行われる。

c）特 許 部（Patent Department）

【例　文】

One expert in the field of corporate patents points out that patent departments sometimes report to the general counsel on the theory that patents are a legal matter. In other cases, they may report to the research director on the theory that patents are the results of research. Or they may report to the company president on the　theory that patents are property.

The Patent Department at ABC, headed for the past 32 years by J B, happens to be in the Legal Division, but no one, least of all the patent attorneys, is unaware of the fact that patents come from research and that they represent a valuable company property.

【語句の説明】

the field of corporate patents：法人関係の特許分野

the general counsel：法務部門の長；counselだけでも法務部長を意味する。

on the theory：理屈で

patents are a legal matte：特許が法的問題である

the research director：研究担当の取締役

patents are the results of research：特許は研究の成果である

headed：指揮を執った；同じ部長でもpatent managerは管理職のニュアンスが強く，patent counselだと特許専門家としてのニュアンスが強い。両者を兼ねそなえたのがheadのようである。

is unaware of the fact～：～いう事実に気づかない

patents come from research：特許は研究から生まれる

they represent a valuable company property：それが価値ある会社の資産を意味する

第1節　法務部門(Legal Division)の組織と活動

---【訳　文】---

　法人関係の特許分野における一人の専門家が次のことを指摘している。すなわち，特許部というのは時によっては特許が法的問題であるという理屈で，法務部門の長の命にしたがい，また他の場合には，特許は研究の成果であるという理屈で，研究担当の取締役の命にしたがうかもしれないし，あるいは特許部が特許は資産であるという理屈で会社の社長の命に服するかもしれない。

　わが社の特許部はJB副社長が過去32年間その指揮を執ってきたが，たまたま法務部門に属している。しかし，誰でも，少なくとも全ての特許弁護士が特許は研究から生まれ，かつそれが価値ある会社の資産を意味するという事実に気づかない者はいない。

---【例　文】---

　A patent is a legal monopoly granted to an inventor by the government which allows the inventor to prevent others from copying or practicing his invention for a specific period of time.

　There may have been a time when most inventions were made by the eccentric genius working in his basement or attic at night. No more, however. Most inventions today come out of research laboratories equipped with the complex tools and the interdisciplinary teams of experts who make modern inventions possible.

　The new techniques have been productive. In the past 50 years, the number of patents issued each year has increased about 50 percent. The number of chemical patents, however, has increased several hundred percent.

【語句の説明】

a patent is a legal monopoly granted to an inventor：特許は政府により発明者に与えられる法的独占権である

allows the inventor to prevent others from ～：発明者は他人が～したりすることを止めさせることが許される

copying or practicing his invention：その発明を模倣したり，実施したりすること

for a specific period of time：特定の期間

第2章　米国会社の法務部門

come out of research laboratories：研究所から生まれる
equipped with the complex tools：複雑な機器類を備えた
the interdisciplinary teams of experts：統制のとれた研究者のチーム
make modern inventions possible：現代の発明を可能とする
productive：生産に寄与する，生産的

【訳　文】

　特許は政府により発明者に与えられる法的独占権であり，その権利により発明者は他人が特定の期間その発明を模倣したり，実施したりすることを禁止させることが許されている。

　大部分の発明が地下室や屋根裏で夜中に仕事をする変人的天才によりなされた時代があったかもしれない。しかし今日，大部分の発明は複雑な機器類を備えた研究所と現代の発明を可能とする統制のとれた研究者のチームから生まれる。

　新しい技術は生産に寄与するものであった。過去50年において，特許数は約50％増えた。しかも化学関係の特許は数百％増加した。

【例　文】

　The job of a patent attorney (and there are 15 of them in the Patent Department, plus five chemists) begins with an invention in one of the research laboratories. The laboratory notifies the Patent Department, asking that a patent application be considered. The Patent Department, after analyzing the request, may recommend no further action, or it may proceed to obtain a patent.

　Before a patent application is prepared, it is necessary to know "the state of the art" what has been patented and reported previously. Armed with this information, the patent attorney prepares a description of the invention showing how it differs from what preceded it (prior art) and what utility and advantages can be contributed by this difference.

【語句の説明】

patent attorney：特許弁護士（弁護士で特許を扱う資格を有する者）；弁護士ではなくて特許を扱う資格者はpatent agentと解される。
five chemists：5名の化学専門家；実状はそのうちの3名はpatent agent

第1節　法務部門(Legal Division)の組織と活動

a patent application be considered：特許出願の検討する
after analyzing the request：要請を分析した後に
may recommend no further action, or it may proceed to obtain a patent.：さらに仕事を進めるべきでないとの意見を具申するかもしれないし、あるいは特許取得の手続きを勧めるかもしれない
"the state of the art"："技術の状態"
what has been patented and reported previously：以前にどんなものが特許になり報告されているか
armed with this information：この情報で武装して
showing how it differs from what preceded it (prior art)：それが以前から存在したもの(先行技術)といかに異なるかを示す
what utility and advantages can be contributed by this difference：どんな用途および有利性がこの相違によりもたらせられ得るか

【訳　文】

　特許弁護士(そのうちの15名は特許部におり、さらに5名の化学専門家)の仕事は、研究所における一つの発明とともに始まる。研究所は特許部に通知し、特許出願の検討を求めてくる。特許部はその要請を分析した後に、さらに仕事を進めるべきでないとの意見を具申するかもしれないし、あるいは特許取得の手続きを勧めるかもしれない。
　特許出願書類を作成する前に、"技術の状態"－すなわち、以前にどんなものが特許になり報告されているか－を知る必要がある。この情報で武装し、特許弁護士はそれが以前から存在したもの(先行技術)といかに異なるか、ならびにどんな用途および有利性がこの相違によりもたらされるか、ということを示す特許明細書を作成する。

【例　文】

　This description is followed with claims designed to specify the scope of the monopoly requested for the invention. The completed application is then filed in the U.S. Patent Office and ultimately examined by a patent examiner who may either grant the patent or raise objections and criticisms. The patent attorney may then amend the claims or he may argue with the examiner.

23

第2章　米国会社の法務部門

> About three years are generally required to obtain a patent, unless an interference proceeding between two or more applicants is involved, in which case the time may run from five to ten years. 〜

【語句の説明】

this description is followed with claims：この記載の次に特許請求の範囲がくる
designed to specify the scope of the monopoly：独占権の範囲を明示すべき
ultimately examined by a patent examiner：最終的には審査官により審査される
may either grant the patent or raise objections and criticisms：特許を与えるか，あるいは拒絶とその理由を提示するかの何れかをすることができる
amend the claims：特許請求の範囲を補正する
may argue with the examiner：審査官と争う
obtain a patent：特許を取得する
unless an interference proceeding between two or more applicants is involved：2名以上の出願人の間で抵触審査手続きが関係する場合には別で

【訳　文】

　この記載の次に，その発明に基づいて要求する独占権の範囲を明示すべき特許請求の範囲がくる。完成した特許出願書類は米国特許庁に提出され，最終的には審査官により審査され，審査官は特許を与えるか，あるいは拒絶とその理由を提示するかの何れかをすることができる。特許弁護士は，そこで特許請求の範囲を補正し，あるいは審査官と争う。一般的に，約3年が特許を取得するために要求される。ただし，2名以上の出願人の間で抵触審査手続きが関係する場合には別で，その場合にはその期間は5年から10年になるかもしれない。

(第2節 a)(3) 明細書を参照)

　抵触審査手続きが関係した場合には，特許になるのに数十年かかることがある。日本やその他の外国では，特許要件の一つとして先願制度を採用しているが，米国は先発明制度を採用している。そこで，2人以上の発明者のうちで誰が最先の発明者であるかを決める手続きが抵触審査手続きである。これがいわゆるsubmarine 特許の原因をなしている。詳細は別に述べることにする。

第1節　法務部門(Legal Division)の組織と活動

【例　文】

However, the phrase "patent granted" does not necessarily establish an inviolate sanctuary. Competitors may challenge the validity of the boundaries, or they may choose to poach in the forbidden territory. In either case, the company which has been granted the patent may halve to fight hard to keep violators and poachers out, and this too is a part of the work of a patent attorney. As ABC has moved into international commerce, foreign patents have assumed increasing importance. The level of effort in foreign countries is approaching that in the United Slates, according to J B. In one case, patents or registrations were filed by ABC in 88 foreign countries. ABC uses different systems in handling foreign applications. Mostly, cases are filed through attorneys in the foreign country, but the volume of patent work may be sufficient to justify stationing a member of the Patent Department in foreign countries. This is presently the case in the United Kingdom and in Japan.

【語句の説明】

the phrase "patent granted"：〝特許付与〞という言葉

does not necessarily establish an inviolate sanctuary：必ずしも不可侵な聖地を確立しない

competitors may challenge the validity of the boundaries：競業者はその境界線の有効性について争うことができる

they may choose to poach in the forbidden territory：彼らはその禁止された領域内に入ることを選択するかもしれない

in either case：いずれの場合にしろ

has moved into international commerce：国際交易に参加するようになった

have assumed increasing importance：重要性を増した

the level of effort in foreign countries：外国における努力レベル

is approaching that in the United Slates：合衆国におけるレベルに近づいている

uses different systems：異なったシステムを用いる

in handling foreign applications：外国特許出願の扱いについて

the volume of patent work may be sufficient：特許業務の量が充分であるかもし

25

第2章　米国会社の法務部門

れない

to justify stationing a member of the Patent Department in foreign countries：
外国に特許部のメンバーを駐在させることが正当化されるのに

this is presently the case in～：このようなことは現在では～である

【訳　文】

　しかしながら"特許付与"という言葉は，必ずしも不可侵な聖地を確立するわけではない。競業者はその境界線の有効性について争うことができ，あるいは彼らはその禁止された領域内に入ることを選択するかもしれない。いずれの場合にしろ，特許を付与された会社は侵害者を排除するために，強力に闘わなければならないかもしれないし，またこのことが，特許弁護士の仕事の一部でもある。

　わが社が国際交易に参加するようになったことで，外国特許がその重要性を増してきた。外国における努力レベルは，特許担当副社長によれば，合衆国におけるレベルに近づいているとのことである。なおわが社では，ある製品の場合には88ヶ国の外国において，特許あるいは登録の出願をした。

　わが社では外国特許出願の扱いについては，異なるシステムを用いている。大抵は外国にある代理人を通じて出願しているが，特許業務の量からして外国に特許部のメンバーを駐在させることを正当化するには充分であるかもしれない。このようなところは，現在では英国と日本である。

英国および日本ではそれぞれの部員が組織を持ち，英国の駐在員はヨーロッパ諸国および南アの特許を担当している。日本の駐在員もやはり独自の組織を持ち，アジア諸国の特許と日本の特許および法務一般を担当している。

【例　文】

　J B points out that it is extremely desirable for an ABC patent attorney to have degrees in both chemistry and law. "And our attorneys maintain both their technical and legal proficiencies," he says.

　The Patent Department also handles the registration and protection of trademarks. "In general," explains Q, who with E, is concerned with this job, "we object to other companies using 'P＿＿' as part of a trademark for a plastic, or to the use of a 't＿＿' suffix on agricultural products and sanitary

第1節　法務部門（Legal Division）の組織と活動

> chemicals. In both cases these names have become identified with ABC products and, if used for competing products, could create confusion in the mind of the buyer."

【語句の説明】

it is extremely desirable：極めて望ましい
for an ABC patent attorney to have degrees in～：ABCの特許弁護士が～の学位を持つこと
our attorneys maintain both their technical and legal proficiencies：わが社の弁護士は技術と法律の両方の能力を兼ね備えている
the Patent Department also handles～：特許部はまた～の取り扱いをしている
the registration and protection of trademarks：商標の登録と保護
we object to other companies using 'P___' as part of a trademark for a plastic：われわれは他の会社がプラスチックを指定商品とする商標の一部として'P___'を使用することに異議の申し立てをする
these names have become identified with ABC products：これらの名称はABC社の製品を表すと認定されており
if used for competing products：競業製品に使用された場合には
create confusion in the mind of the buyer：購入者の心に混同を生じさせる

―【訳　文】―――――――――――――――――――

　J.B.副社長は次のように指摘している。ABCの特許弁護士は化学と法律の両方の学位を持つことが極めて望ましい。副社長自身の言葉によると，「わが社の弁護士は技術と法律の両方の能力を兼ね備えている。」とのことである。

　特許部は，また商標の登録と保護の取り扱いをしている。E弁護士とともに，この業務を担当しているQ弁護士は「一般的に，われわれは他の会社がプラスチックを指定商品とする商標の一部として'P___'を使用すること，あるいは農業用製品および衛生用化学剤に対して't___'という接尾辞（を有する商標）を使用することに異議申し立てをする。両方の場合において，これらの名称はABC社の製品を表すと認定されており，競業製品に使用された場合には，購入者の心に混同を生じさせる可能性があるからである。」

第2章　米国会社の法務部門

d) 税　務　部（Tax Department）

【例　文】

> The ABC Company Tax Department contains only three professional people, but it's responsible for a whopping chunk of money : 9.5 cents out of every sales dollar, or a total of some $＿＿ million in 19＿＿.
>
> F B, head of the Tax Department, says the basic function of the department is "to see that the company pays all the taxes for which it's liable, but no more." Individual taxpayers are probably correctly convinced that if they owe taxes, somebody is going to tell them about it. This is not true for corporations. A corporation is expected to know the taxes for which it is liable, to be thoroughly familiar with the method of computing them, and to file the returns when due. Largest of the tax bites and largest of the returns to be filed is the federal income tax. This single tax is almost as large as the company's net earnings, and the tax return itself can be better measured in pounds or inches than pages. T F is the department's expert on federal tax programs and returns, but he depends on the Financial Division for much of his information.

【語句の説明】

Tax Department contains only three professional people：税務部はたった3名の専門職で構成されている

responsible for a whopping chunk of money：とんでもない額の責任を負わせる

9.5 cents out of every sales dollar：あらゆる販売金額のうちの9.5セント

the basic function of the department：当部の基本的職掌

the company pays all the taxes：一切の税金を支払う

it's liable：会社が支払う義務のある

individual taxpayers：個人の納税者

probably correctly convinced that：多分，納得するであろう，それは正しいであろう

this is not true for corporations：このことは会社には当てはまらない

a corporation is expected to know the taxes：会社は支払うべき税金について知ることが期待されている

第 1 節　法務部門 (Legal Division) の組織と活動

be thoroughly familiar with the method of computing them：その計算方法を完全に熟知する
to file the returns when due：期限には申告書を提出する
largest of the tax bites：税額がもっとも大きいのは
largest of the returns to be filed：申告額がもっとも大きいのは
this single tax is almost as large as the company's net earnings：この単独の税金は会社の純利益とほとんど同額である
can be better measured in pounds or inches than pages：頁数よりもポンド(重さ)やインチ(大きさ)でより良く測りうる；いかに税金の申告書が膨大なものであるかの表現。

──【訳　文】──

　税務部は，たった3名の専門職で構成されている。しかし，とんでもない額の金銭；あらゆる販売金額のうち9.5セント，すなわち19___年では___千億ドルの全額に対して責任を負っている。

　税務部長であるFB氏は，当部の基本的職掌は「会社が支払う義務のある一切の税金を支払うが，しかしそれ以上は払わない。」と言っている。個人の納税者は多分，彼らが税金を支払わなければならない場合には，誰かがそれについて話してくれるだろうということで納得するだろうし，それは正しいであろう。しかし，このことは会社には当てはまらない。会社は支払うべき税金について知り，その計算方法を完全に熟知し，期限には申告書を提出することが期待されている。

　税額がもっとも大きくかつ申告額も大きいのは，連邦所得税である。この単独の税金は会社の純利益とほとんど同額であり，その納税書それ自体は頁数よりもポンド(重さ)やインチ(大きさ)で測った方がよいほどである。

　TF氏は当部の連邦税金プログラムと申告の専門家であるが，しかしその情報の多くは財務部に頼っている。

──【例　文】──

　What they lack in individual size, the local and state tax returns make up in numbers. B P spends his time preparing these local and state returns-some 350 of them each year.

第2章　米国会社の法務部門

The members of the Tax Department also serve as consultants, If the company wishes to establish a branch sales office in a state where it is not presently doing business, for instance, one of the first steps would be to make an investigation of the probable tax liability arising from a multitude of different taxes. These might include income (similar to the federal income tax), franchise (a tax on the privilege of engaging in business), excise (a special tax which may be levied on the value of property such as land, buildings, inventories, etc.), and sales, use, and property taxes. In some cases, the taxes might be greater than the profits produced by a small sales office, and this factor would obviously weigh heavily in the decision to establish such an office.

【語句の説明】

what they lack in individual size：個別的な大きさの点では劣ること
the local and state tax returns make up in numbers：地方税と州税の申告はその数の点で引けはとらない
preparing these local and state returns：これらの地方税と州税の申告準備をする
serve as consultants：コンサルタントとしての役割を果たす
if the company wishes to establish a branch sales office：会社が営業支店を設けよと希望する場合には
in a state where it is not presently doing business：会社が現在業務を行っていない州に
one of the first steps would be to ～：最初のステップの一つは～である
make an investigation of the probable tax liability：蓋然的税額について調査する
franchise (a tax on the privilege of engaging in business:)：事業免許税（業務に従事する特権に対する税金）
excise (a special tax which may be levied on ～)：資産税（～に課税されるかもしれない特別税）
the value of property such as land, buildings, inventories, etc.：土地，建物，棚卸し資産等のような資産の価値
sales, use, and property taxes：販売税，使用税および財産税
greater than the profits produced by a small sales office：小さな販売所からの利

第 1 節　法務部門（Legal Division）の組織と活動

益よりも大きい

this factor would obviously weigh heavily in the decision ～ ：この要素が～を決定に当たり，大きなウエイトを占めることは明らかである

to establish such an office ：このような販売所を設けること

---【訳　文】---

　個別的な大きさの点では劣るが，地方税と州税の申告はその数の点で引けを取らない。BP氏は，その時間をこれらの地方税と州税の申告準備－毎年約350種－に費やしている。

　税務部のメンバーはまたコンサルタントとしての役割を果たす。会社が現在業務を行っていない州に営業支店を設けようと希望する場合には，たとえば最初のステップの一つは多数の異なる税金から発生する蓋然的税額について調査することである。これらには所得税（連邦所得税と類似），事業免許税（業務に従事する特権に対する税金），資産税（土地，建物，棚卸し資産等のような資産の価値に基づいて課税されるかも知れない特別税）ならびに販売税，使用税および財産税などを含む。ある場合には，税金は小さな販売所からの利益よりも大きくなることがあるかも知れないし，この要素がこのような販売所を設ける決定に当たり，大きなウエイトを占めることは明らかである。

---【例　文】---

　F points out that the company does not lobby to obtain special tax treatment, but it does have a real interest in the development of logical, rational tax laws. To further this work, F serves as a member of the Tax Committee of the Philadelphia Chamber of Commerce and a member of the Manufacturing Chemists Association Tax Policy Committee. When the occasion warrants, F has appeared before appropriate government bodies as an expert witness.

【語句の説明】

the company does not lobby to obtain special tax treatment ：会社は税制上特別の取り扱いをうけるためにロビー活動はしない

it does have a real interest in the development of logical, rational tax laws ：論理的にして合理的な税法の開発について強く興味を持っている

31

第2章　米国会社の法務部門

to further this work：この仕事をさらに進めるため

the Tax Committee of the Philadelphia Chamber of Commerce：フィラデルフィア商工会議所の税務委員会

the Manufacturing Chemists Association Tax Policy Committee：化学品製造業者組合税務政策委員会

when the occasion warrants：(特別な事情)必要がある時に

F has appeared before appropriate government bodies：F弁護士は以前に政府のしかるべき団体に出頭したことがある

as an expert witness：鑑定人として

---【訳　文】---

　同部の部長であるF弁護士は，次のことを指摘している。すなわち，会社は税制上特別の取り扱いをうけるためにロビー活動はしないが，論理的にして合理的な税法の開発について強く興味を持っていることは事実である。この仕事をさらに進めるため，F弁護士はフィラデルフィア商工会議所の税務委員会のメンバーおよび化学品製造業者組合税務政策委員会のメンバーになっている。事情があり，F弁護士は鑑定人として以前に政府のしかるべき団体に出頭したことがある。

---

e）保　険　部（Insurance Department）

---【例　文】---

　EM is a man who buys insurance in very large chunks. EM is head of the Insurance Department, although to many people he is the "benefits man. This is understakable, since many of the company's benefit programs are related to insurance. Loss visible is the department's corporate insurance program. E M defines the two principal divisions of activity as "corporate insurance and social insurance." The corporate Insurance, he says, concerns things; the social insurance concerns people.

【語句の説明】

buys insurance in very large chunks：非常に大規模な保険をかける

第1節　法務部門(Legal Division)の組織と活動

head of the Insurance Department：保険部の部長
the "benefits man"："給付人"
the company's benefit programs：会社の給付プログラム
related to insurance：保険と関係している
loss visible：見える損失
defines the two principal divisions of activity as ～：二つの主要な活動部門を～と定義づける
corporate insurance and social insurance：法人保険と社会保険

【訳　文】

　EM弁護士は，非常に大規模な保険をかける人である。また，同弁護士は保険部の部長である。もっとも彼は，多くの人にとっては"給付人"である。このことは理解できるが，それは会社の給付プログラムの多くは保険と関係しているからである。見える損失が会社の保険プログラムである。同弁護士は，二つの主要な活動部門を「法人保険と社会保険」と定義づけている。法人保険とは物に関するものであり，社会保険とは人間に関するものであると，彼は言っている。

【例　文】

　EM joined ABC Company in 19＿＿ to handle insurance matters. He later became the first employee in a new Insurance Department, and one of his first assignments was to work on a ABC Company Pension Plan. Since then his field of responsibility has increased markedly. Today, in addition to the pension plan, there is group life, travel accident, accident and sickness, medical, and expanded workmen's compensation and social security benefits, all under the umbrella of what EM calls social insurance. In addition, various corporate insurance programs are handled largely by HT, assistant department manager.

【語句の説明】
joined ABC Company in 1995 to handle insurance matters：1995年保険業務を扱うためにABC社に入社した
became the first employee in a new Insurance Department：新しい保険部の最

第2章　米国会社の法務部門

初の従業員となった

one of his first assignments was to work on a ABC Company Pension Plan：最初に割り当てられた仕事の一つは，ABC社の会社年金計画を策定することであった

his field of responsibility has increased markedly：彼の責任分野は顕著に拡大した

in addition to the pension plan：年金計画のほかに

group life：団体生命

travel accident：旅行保険

accident and sickness：傷害・疾病

medical：医療

expanded workmen's compensation：拡大された労働者補償

social security：社会年金

benefits：給付

all under the umbrella of ～：すべて～の傘下にある

EM calls social insurance：EM弁護士が社会保険と呼ぶ

various corporate insurance programs：会社の種々の保険プログラム

handled largely by HT, assistant department manager：主に次長であるHT弁護士により取り扱われている

【訳　文】

　EM弁護士は，1995年保険業務を扱うためにABC社に入社した。後に，彼は新しい保険部の最初の従業員となり，最初に割り当てられた仕事の一つは，ABC社の会社年金計画を策定することであった。それ以来，彼の責任分野は顕著に拡大した。今日では年金計画のほかに，団体生命，旅行，傷害・疾病，医療および拡大された労働者補償，社会年金給付，これらはすべてEM弁護士が社会保険と呼ぶ傘下にある。さらに，会社の種々の保険プログラムは，主に次長であるHT弁護士により取り扱われている。

【例　文】

　With many of the social insurance programs, ABC Company acts as more than a simple purchaser of a standard insurance policy. For instance, the pension plan funds were originally placed with a life insurance company which guaranteed a minimum return. As this program was reviewed from time to time, it became

第1節　法務部門(Legal Division)の組織と活動

> apparent that inflation would cut deeply into the purchasing power of the money when it was paid out in the form of benefits. Therefore, in 1995, the decision was made to invest part of the funds in equities.

【語句の説明】
acts as ～：～としての役割を果たす
more than a simple purchaser of a standard insurance policy：標準的な保険証券の単なる購入者たるを超える
for instance：例えば
the pension plan funds：年金計画の資金
were originally placed with a life insurance company：もとは生命保険会社にまかせられていた
guaranteed a minimum return：最低額のリターンを保証していた
this program was reviewed from time to time：このプログラムは時々検討された
became apparent：明らかになった
inflation would cut deeply into the purchasing power of the money：インフレーションがその購買力を大きく減少させるだろう
when it was paid out in the form of benefits：給付の形で支払われるときに
the decision was made to invest part of the funds：資金の一部を投資する決定がなされた
in equities：株式に

【訳　文】
　多くの社会保険プログラムについて，会社は標準的な保険証券の単なる購入者たるを超える役割を果たしている。例えば，年金計画の資金はもともとは生命保険会社にまかせられたものであり，それは最低額のリターンを保証していた。このプログラムは時々検討されたことにより，インフレーションにより給付の形で支払われるときには，その購買力が大きく減少することが明らかになった。そこで1995年に資金の一部を株式投資にする決定がなされた。

第2章　米国会社の法務部門

【例　文】

　EM and other members of corporate management maintain a constant review of benefit programs, and EM spends a lot of time talking with insurance salesmen, keeping up to date on changes in insurance patterns and alert to ways in which he can buy the most protection for the least money.

　HT is the expert on corporate insurance. Unlike some of the social insurance programs, the corporate insurance is primarily to protect against risks which could have a significant effect on the ability of the company to continue operation. The company takes this insurance for exactly the same reason an individual insures his home against fire loss. The possibility that anyone's home will burn is low, but at the same time no one could afford the large loss. Neither can ABC Company. Neither, in fact, can any one insurance company -- the company's insurance is handled through insurance associations or through re-insurance by groups of companies.

【語句の説明】

members of corporate management：企業管理担当のメンバー

maintain a constant review of benefit programs：給付プログラムについて常に検討する

EM spends a lot of time talking with insurance salesmen：EM弁護士は保険会社の担当者との会議に長い時間を費やす

keeping up to date on changes in insurance patterns：保険形態の変化に遅れないようにする

alert to ways：方法に注意を払っている

the most protection for the least money：最小の費用で最高の保護

unlike some of the social insurance programs：社会保険プログラムとは異なり

the corporate insurance is primarily to protect against risks：法人保険は，本来，リスクに対して保護することである

could have a significant effect on ～：～に大きな影響を有しているはずであった

the ability of the company to continue operation：会社の業務継続能力

takes this insurance：この保険をかける

第1節 法務部門(Legal Division)の組織と活動

for exactly the same reason an individual insures his home against fire loss：個人が自分の家を火災による損害に対して保険をかけるのと全く同じ理由で

the possibility that anyone's home will burn is low：誰の家でも燃えるだろうと言う可能性は低い

but at the same time：しかし同時に

no one could afford the large loss：誰もその大きな損失を負担する能力はない

neither can ABC Company：ABC社だとてない

neither, in fact, can any one insurance company：事実，どんな保険会社でも単独でその能力はないはずである

the company's insurance is handled：その会社の保険は取り扱われる

through insurance associations or through re-insurance by groups of companies：保険組合あるいは会社グループによる再保険により

【訳　文】

　EM弁護士とその他の企業管理担当のメンバーが給付プログラムについて常に検討しており，EM弁護士は保険会社の担当者との会議に長い時間を費やして保険形態の変化に遅れないようにし，また最小の費用で最高の保護を受けられる方法に注意を払っている。

　HT弁護士は法人保険の専門家である。社会保険プログラムとは異なり，法人保険は，本来，リスクに対して保護することであり，リスクは会社の業務継続能力に大きな影響を有しているはずであった。会社は個人が自分の家を火災による損害に対して保険をかけるとの全く同じ理由で，この保険をかける。誰の家でも燃えるだろうと言う可能性は低いが，しかし同時に，誰もその大きな損失を負担する能力はない。ABC社だとてない。事実，どんな保険会社でも単独でその能力はないはずであり，その会社の保険は保険組合あるいは会社グループによる再保険により取り扱われている。

【例　文】

　On new construction, the Insurance Department becomes involved when projects are on the drawing board. Insurance rates are negotiated during the engineering design, and changes can be made in plant design which will have an important bearing on rates.

第2章　米国会社の法務部門

> Business interruption is an important part of the total package of risk protection. If a major unit at one of the ABC Company plants was destroyed, hazard insurance would pay for its replacement, but it would not pay for the loss of production which might be considerably greater than the value of the unit itself. Therefore, business interruption insurance is very important.

【語句の説明】

on new construction：新しい建設工事に関しては

the Insurance Department becomes involved：保険部が関係してくる

when projects are on the drawing board：プロジェクトが製図板上にあるときに

insurance rates are negotiated during the engineering design：保険料率は構築（エンジニァリング）設計中に交渉の対象とされる

changes can be made in plant design：プラント設計を変更することができる

will have an important bearing on rates.：料率に重要な影響のあるであろう

business interruption：業務中断

an important part of the total package of risk protection：リスク保護トータルパッケージ中の重要な一部

if a major unit at one of the ABC Company plants was destroyed：ABC工場の一つにある主要なユニットが破壊された場合には

hazard insurance would pay for its replacement：危険保険はその代換え品の支払いをするであろう

it would not pay for the loss of production：その製造品に係る損失はカバーしない

might be considerably greater than the value of the unit itself：そのユニットの価値自体よりもかなり大きいかもしれない

business interruption insurance is very important：業務中断に関する保険は非常に重要である

【訳　文】

　新しい建設工事に関しては、プロジェクトが製図板上にあるときに保険部が関係してくる。保険料率は構築(エンジニアリング)設計中に交渉の対象とされ、料率に重要な影響のあるプラント設計を変更することができる。

　業務中断は、リスク保護トータルパッケージ中の重要な一部である。ABC

第1節　法務部門（Legal Division）の組織と活動

工場の一つにある主要なユニットが破壊された場合には，危険保険はその代換え品の支払いをするであろうが，その製造品に係る損失はカバーしないので，その損失はそのユニットの価値自体よりもかなり大きいかもしれない。したがって，業務中断に関する保険は非常に重要である。

f）法務部門の究極の目的 — 再び上席副社長の言葉

【例　文】

"An overall function of the Legal Division," says FH, "is to minimize risks wherever possible. ABC Company policy leaves no doubt about its intent to operate within the letter and the spirit of the law whether in the case of product liability, patent protection, employee benefits or compensation, tax obligations, marketing or any other matter."

In its relations to other departments, the Legal Division most often acts in a service capacity. It provides information; it interprets the law; it assists in procedures of various legal actions. "We have no prima donnas in the Legal Division" comments FH. "We are here simply to serve the best interests of the company in its legal relations."

【語句の説明】

An overall function of the Legal Division：法務部門全体としての職務
to minimize risks wherever possible：可能な限りリスクを最小限にすること
ABC Company policy leaves no doubt about its intent：ABC社の方針はその意図に対して疑いを残さないようにする
to operate within the letter and the spirit of the law：法の意味と精神の範囲内において操業する
product liability：製造物責任
patent protection：特許による保護
employee benefits or compensation：従業員の給付あるいは報酬
tax obligations：税の負担
marketing or any other matter：市場開発あるいはその他の事項

39

第2章　米国会社の法務部門

in its relations to other departments：他の部との関連において
most often acts in a service capacity：サービス的立場で行動することが最も多い
provide information：情報を与える
interpret the law：法を解釈する
assist in procedures of various legal actions：種々の法的行為の手続きに関して援助する
comments：説明する
serve the best interests of the company in its legal relations：その法的関係において会社の最大利益のために奉仕する

【訳　文】

　再び上席副社長のことばを示す。「法務部門全体としての職務は，可能な限りリスクを最小限にすることである。ABC社の方針は製造物責任の場合であろうと，特許による保護，あるいは従業員の給付あるいは報酬，税の負担，市場開発，あるいはその他の事項であろうと，法の意味と精神の範囲内において操業する意図に対して疑いを残さないようにすることである。」

　他の部との関連において，法務部門はサービス的立場で行動することが最も多い。法務部門は，情報を与え，法を解釈し，種々の法的行為の手続きに関して援助する。さらに同上席副社長は次のように説明している。

　「法務部門にはプリマドンナはいない。われわれは，ここではその法的関係において会社の最大利益のために奉仕することだけである。」

第2節　特許と英語

a) 特許関係の英語
(1) 特許の英語

特許関係の英文書類には，やたらと特殊の法律用語と技術用語が使用されている。また手続き関係の書式もいろいろとある。例えば，特許出願書，明細書，図面，審査請求書，種々の意見書，申立書，答弁書などがある。しかし国際業務で英語の知識をもっとも必要とするのは，特許などの出願書に添付する明細書であろう。この明細書は，発明内容を開示する技術文書の部分と発明内容の開示の代償として要求する権利の範囲に係る法的文書の部分よりなると言われている。

(2) 特許制度

まずこの明細書で使用する英語の説明にはいる前に，その前提をなしている特許制度についてごく簡単にふれる。

特許制度の目的は，有益な発明をした者が，その発明を公表し世人に利用させる機会を与えることを奨励し，産業の発達を図ることである。そこで，発明者に発明の開示を奨励するための手段として，発明開示の代償として発明者に対して特権を与えることにしている。その特権とは，一定期間，発明者等だけにその発明を独占的に利用する機会を与え，特別の利益を受けることを内容としている。

(3) 明　細　書

明細書の話に戻る。発明者は，発明の内容に対して，ともすれば大きすぎる権利を要求しがちである。特許庁は公益の立場から，発明者(出願者)の要求を発明の内容にふさわしい大きさの特権に相応するように調整せんと努め，このようにして発明者の利益と公共の利益とのバランスをはかっていいる。

特許庁の審査官は，特許要件−発明を構成するか否か，新規性や進歩性があるか否かなど−を審査する。「OK.」なら出願公告の決定をなし，その結果第三者に対して異議申し立ての機会を与えるために出願内容が特許公報に公告される。ここでの争いの要点は，発明内容が特許要件を満たしているか否か，発明が特許要件を満たしているとしても，その請求範囲は妥当なものであるか否かということである。

また，審査官は特許阻害事由があれば「拒絶理由」を出して出願人に意見書を提出する機会を与える。

出願人は，出願が拒絶になった場合には，拒絶査定不服審判の請求をし，審判の結果に不服なら，東京高等裁判所に訴えることができる。

(4) 明細書の翻訳

国際関係の特許業務では，英文で書かれた明細書を読んだり書いたりすることが中心である。出願拒絶や異議申し立てにおける立論において常に考慮するのは明細書の内容である。先に述べた如く，明細書は技術的部分と法律的部分からなり，前者は技術内容開示の部分であり，後者は特許請求の範囲であると言われている。もっとも技術内容の開示部分にも「**broadening paragraph**」と呼ばれる法的部分もある。これらの詳細については，別に「許明細書の読み方・書き方」の中で言及するつもりである。

b) 特許明細書
(1) 超ミニ米国特許明細書（英文和訳）

特許明細書を作成する専門家は弁理士であるが，ごく大ざっぱに言うと法律系の弁理士は意匠，商標の業務を取り扱い，技術系の弁理士が特許，実用新案の業務を取り扱っている。さらに技術系弁理士の業務は，機械，電気，化学の専門分野に分かれていると言われている。しかし現在では，技術分野は高度に細分化され，有機化学とか無機化学とかの分野というのは意味をなさず，大事務所に勤務する弁理士は，さらに細分化された専門業務を担当している。したがって，具体的な特許明細書を例示して英語について説明しようとしても，どんな明細書を使用したらよいのか，その選択は大変難しい。明細書によっては，大変ページ数の多いものもあり，ひとつの特許を公開するのに数冊の特許公報を要し，翻訳料が数百万円になったと聞いたことがある。そこで，本書の性格上，短くかつ技術内容の簡単なものを選択しなければならない。ところが，偶然その目的にぴったりの明細書を入手することができたので，例文として紹介する。

ところで，米国の特許明細書と言うと大抵長文なものと相場が決まっているように思われる。少なくともわが国の特許明細書，特に実用新案のそれよりは長いの

が普通であり、米国特許の明細書で1ページのものなどは到底考えることができない。ところが偶然にも,本文がわずか12行半で書かれており,特許請求の範囲が1行半よりなる超ミニ特許明細書にお目にかかったのである。それは、米国特許第2,649,367号（1953年8月18日）である。このように特許番号が付いているのであるから,本物である。

この「ミニ」明細書にお目にかかった経緯は、某翻訳協会より米国の化学,薬剤,合金関係の特許明細書の訳読の講義をするよう依頼され、それで米国のPatent Attorneyに参考となる明細書のサンプルを送ってくれるようにお願いした。同氏は、化学に関する発明についての代表的な明細書を15通送ってくれたはずなのだが,1通が見当たらず探したところ、たった1枚の紙きれの真ん中に少し記載されているだけの明細書が見つかった。それが明細書とは思わず、他の明細書の附属書類か何かと間違えてしまったからである。

日本の特許明細書には
 ① 発明の名称
 ② 図面の簡単な説明
 ③ 発明の詳細な説明
 ④ 特許請求の範囲
を記載しなくてはならないことになっており、アメリカの特許明細書には、次の事項を記載しなくてはならないこととされている。

 ① 発明の名称　　　　　　　（Title of Invention）
 ② 技術内容を開示する要約　（Abstract of the Disclosure）
 ③ 関係出願に対するクロス－レファレンス（もしあるとすれば）
 　　　　　　　　　　　　　（cross-reference to related applications, if any）
 ④ 発明の簡単な要約　　　　（brief summary of the invention）
 ⑤ 図面があるときは、図面の簡単な説明
 　　　　　　　　　　　　　（brief description of the several views of the drawings, if there are drawings）
 ⑥ 発明の詳細な説明　　　　（detailed description of the invention）
 ⑦ 1または2以上のクレーム（claim or claims）
 ⑧ 署　　名　　　　　　　　（signature）

ところが、これから紹介する「ミニ」特許明細書は、その本文がわずか12行半

よりなるにもかかわらず、米国特許法で要求される明細書の記載要件を充足しているのである。もっとも、1953年8月18日に特許されたものであるから、上述②と③の「技術内容を開示する要約」と「関係出願に対するクロス－レファレンス」が本明細書に記載されていない。

まず、その明細書を縮小して全体像を示す。次にその明細書を、a．書誌部、b．主要部－技術内容の開示と請求範囲、c．引例部に分解し、それぞれを拡大して示し解説する。

〈明細書の全体像〉

UNITED STATES PATENT OFFICE
2,649,367
CADMIUM-FREE LOW FUSING POINT ALLOY
Albert A. Smith, Jr., Metuchen, and John L. Everhart, Linden, N. J., assignors to American Smelting and Refining Company, New York, N. Y., a corporation of New Jersey
No Drawing. Application October 7, 1950, Serial No.189,044
1 Claim. (Cl.75-134)

1

This invention relates to alloys and more particularly to low fusing point alloys.

It is an object of the invention to provide cadmium-free, low melting point alloys.

In accordance with the invention, alloys are provided comprising, by weight, 32-34 % Bi, 42-44 % In, 7-8 % Pb and 15-18 % Sn, and have fusing points of approximately 59 ℃.

It will be observed from the compositions that these alloys do not contain cadmium and, accordingly, they are particularly suitable for certain applications as heat transfer media. where cadmium would be detrimental.

What is claimed is:

Low melting point alloys composed of 32-34 % Bi, 42-44 % In, 7-8 % Pb and 15-18 % Sn.

ALBERT A. SMITH, JR.
JOHN L., EVERHART.

2

References Cited in the file of this patent

UNITED STATES PATENT

Number	Name	Date
2,218,153	Pray _____	Oct. 15, 1940

OTHER REFERENCES

French, Industrial and Engineering Chemistry, vol. 27, December 1935; pages 1464 and 1465.

Smith, Metal Industry, October 26, 1945; page 262.

" Fusible Alloys Containing Tin," September 1949, 24 pages, page 3 relied on. Published by the Tin Research Institute, Columbus, Ohio.

a．書誌部

【例文】

UNITED STATES PATENT OFFICE

2,649,367

CADMIUM-FREE LOW FUSING POINT ALLOY

———————，———————

N. J., assignors to American
A and B Company, New York,
N. Y., a corporation of New Jersey
No Drawing. Application October 7, 1950,
Serial No.189,044
1 Claim. (Cl. 75 － 134)

【訳文】

米 国 特 許 庁

第 2,649367 号

カドミウムを含有しない低融点合金

発　明　者　：（省略）
譲渡先(出願人)：ニューヨーク州ニューヨーク市，ニュージャーシ州法人，
　　　　　　　　Ａ＆Ｂ　Co.,Ltd.
添 付 図 面：なし
出　願　日　：1950年10月7日
出 願 番 号　：189,044
クレーム数　：1
分 類 番 号　：75 － 134

第2章　米国会社の法務部門

b．主要部－技術内容の開示と請求範囲

【例　文】

　This invention relates to alloys and more particularly to low fusing point alloys.

　It is an object of the invention to provide cadmium-free, low melting point alloys.

　In accordance with the invention, alloys are provided comprising, by weight, 32〜34％ Bi, 42〜44％ In, 7〜8％ Pb and 15〜18％ Sn, and have fusing points of approximately 59℃.

　It will be observed from the compositions that these alloys do not contain cadmium and, accordingly, they are particularly suitable for certain applications as heat transfer media where cadmium would be detrimental.

　What is claimed is:

　Low melting point alloys composed of 32〜34％ Bi, 42〜44％ In, 7〜8％ Pb and 15〜18％ Sn.

【訳　文】

　発明の名称：カドミウムを含有しない低融点合金本発明は合金に関し，さらに詳細に述べれば，低融点合金に関する。本発明の目的は，カドミウムを含有しない砥融点合金を供給することにある。

　本発明によれば，重量で32〜34％のBi，42〜44％のIn，7〜8％のPbおよび15〜18％のSnよりなり，約59℃の融点を有する合金が供給される。

　この合金はカドミウムを含有していない。したがって，それは伝熱導体（heat transfer media）として，カドミウムが害になるような一定の場合に使用するのに特に適していることが，その構成物から認められるであろう。

　特許請求の範囲：32〜34％のBi，42〜44％のIn，7〜8％のPbおよび15〜18％のSnからなる低融点合金。

第2節 特許と英語

c．引例部

【例　文】

References Cited in the file of this patent

UNITED STATES PATENTS

Number	Name	Date
2,218,153	Pray	Oct. 15, 1940

OTHER REFERENCES

FB, Industrial and Engineering Chemistry, vol. 27, December 1935; pages 1464 and 1465.

S, Metal Industry, October 26, 1945; page 262.

"Fusible Alloys Containing Tin," September 1949, 24 pages, page 3 relied on. Published by the Tin Research Institute, Columbus, Ohio.

【訳　文】

本特許のファイル中の引例文献

　　　　米国特許：特許番号　　第2,218,153号
　　　　　　　　発明者　　　　プレイ
　　　　　　　　特許日　　　　1840年10月15日

その他の引例

FBエンジニアリング・ケミストリー
　vol. 27，1935年12月，1464-1465頁
S.，メタル・インダストリー，1945年10月26日，262頁
"錫を含有する易融合金"，1949年9月，24頁，5頁を依拠，錫研究所(オハイオ州，コロンブス)出典

47

第2章 米国会社の法務部門

〈弁理士のコメント〉

　弁理士の某氏によると，このような短い外国の特許明細書は，特許事務所にとつて大変に好ましいとのことである。もっとも営業的に好ましくないのは15頁の外国文の明細書とのことであるが，悪いことには，この15頁位の明細書が多いのである。

　なぜ短い明細書は営業的に好ましいかと言うと，明細書の頁数の多い少ないにかかわらず出願手数料は一定しており，明細書の頁数が少なければそれだけ手数がかからないからである。明細書の頁は，多いのならば徹底して多ければ翻訳料を稼ぐことができるはずである。ここで紹介したような短い特許明細書であれば，1日に何十通もの明細書をつくることができるであろう。

(2) 算盤に関する特許（和文英訳と英文和訳）

　特許の業務は一般的に三つに分かれていて，それは機械，電気，化学であると言われている。しかし，実務上はもっと細かく専門化されているのが実状である。

　本項では，わが国の最も伝統的な製品である算盤をとりあげ，特許に関する英文研究の資料とする。

　資料は若干古くさい特許用語で書かれているが，使用されている言葉は，決して研究資料としての価値を低下させるものではない。実際に，特許異議申し立てや無効審判の手続きにおいて，公告された発明や特許発明の特許性を否認する資料として利用される公知資料のなかには，古い技術文献や特許公報などが使用されることが多くある。むしろ貴重な資料であり，現在でも充分に和文英訳の資料として研究価値があるはずである。ただ，一つ一つのセンテンスがやたらに長く句点などがほとんどないので，英訳にかかる前に，日本文の係り結びをよく把握する必要もある。また，本資料を逐語的に直訳することは不可能であろう。したがって，英訳するには個々の単語や語句を単純に英単語や英語句に入れ替えする作業でなく，日本語の意味内容を英語でどのように表現するかが重要である。

　まず，第1節の「特許関係の英語　a) 特許の英語」で述べたように，特許明細書は技術的文書と法的文書からなるが，技術的文書とは，具体的には特許法第36条第2項に示されている「発明の詳細な説明」に該当し，法的文書とは特許請求の

第2節　特許と英語

範囲である。さらに発明の詳細な説明には，発明の目的，構成，効果について記載することになっている。そこで，米国特許取得の母体となった日本文の技術文書中の目的，構成および効果に関する部分の一部を適宜選び出し，それに適当な見出しを付けて和文英訳の資料として使用する。

また，日本文技術資料から，米国特許の中の「Abstract of the disclosure」，「特許請求の範囲」および「書誌的事項」の部分を逆に資料として英文和訳の解説をする。

なお，本項の最後に当該日本語資料に基づいて取得された米国特許を縮刷して全体像を示す。

a．和文英訳
① 目　　的

【例　文】

　この発明はマグネットを使用したソロバンに関するもので少々の震動を与えてもあるいは傾斜にしても珠崩れせず通常の計算に使用できることは勿論盲人用ソロバンとしても最適であることを特徴とするものである。

【語句の説明】

この発明：this invention

ソロバン：abacus という言葉もあるが，その概念を明確に表現できない懸念もあるので，あえて soroban と訳し，ソロバンを定義づける次のようなセンテンスを加えた。The term "soroban" as used herein denotes "abacus" and the like.

マグネットを使用したソロバン：直訳なら soroban involving the use of magnet であるが，magnetic "soroban" とする。

少々の震動：直訳すると a slight shock であるが，前後関係から考えて a considerable shock とする。

傾斜にしても：even when ～ is placed in a gradient manner

珠崩れせず：not disorderly positioned

通常の計算に使用：for ordinary calculation and computation

盲人用ソロバン：for use by blind people

最適である：直訳すると most suitable であるが，特許文書の慣例を考えて particularly suitable とする。

49

第 2 章　米国会社の法務部門

～を特徴とする：is characterized by（あるいは in that）～

―【訳　文】―――――――――――――――――――――――――
　This invention relates to a magnetic soroban. The term "soroban" as used herein denotes "abacus" and the like. The invention is characterized in that the beads of the soroban are not disorderly positioned even when a considerable shock is given to the soroban or the soroban is placed in a gradient manner. It is particularly suitable as a soroban for use by blind people as well as for ordinary calculation and computation.
――――――――――――――――――――――――――――――

②　構成－1

―【例　文】―――――――――――――――――――――――――
　本発明は金属，合成樹脂，木等で製した横長浅底の箱体に短辺部が珠褶動巾の略々2倍巾の長方形状のマグネチック薄板体をその長辺部を縦方向に当設し，その上に透磁性の薄板を重合し，さらにその上に横方向に一本の梁板を，縦方向に適数の珠褶動棒を設け，該珠褶動棒に磁石に対して吸着性を有する珠を挿嵌してなるものである。
――――――――――――――――――――――――――――――

【語句の説明】
金属，合成樹脂，木等：metal, synthetic resin, wood, etc.
横長浅底の箱体：rectangular tray
短辺部：the shorter sides
珠褶動巾の略々2倍巾：「褶動」は，特に意味がないのでその部分の英訳を省略して approximately twice as wide as the beads. とする。
長方形状のマグネチック薄板体：rectangular magnetic sheets
長辺部を縦方向に当設し：the longer sides of which are kept in touch with each other
その上に透磁性の薄板を重合し：「重合し」は，化学の文献ではないので polimerizet とはしないで，単純に「重ね合わす」と解し place over～とする。したがって，この部分は a film having magnetic permeability placed over said sheets とする。また「その上に」を over them ではなく over said sheets とする。
横方向に一本の梁板：a beam placed along one of the longer sides
縦方向に適数の珠褶動棒を設け：a proper number of bead-travelling rods arranged

over
該珠褶動棒に：on the said bead-travelling rods
磁石に対して吸着性を有する珠：beads sensitive to magnetism
〜を挿嵌してなるものである：〜 set on

【訳　文】

The present invention comprises a rectangular tray made of such material as,for example, metal, synthetic resin, wood, etc., rectangular magnetic sheets placed therein the shorter sides of which are approximately twice as wide as the beads and ,the longer sides of which are kept in touch with each other and, a film having magnetic permeability placed over said sheets, a beam placed along one of the longer sides of the tray, a proper number of bead-travelling rods arranged over the tray and beads sensitive to magnetism set on the said bead-travelling rods.

---

③　構成－2

【例　文】

　　本発明は以上のような欠点を消却してなるものでマグネチック薄板の吸引力を平均させることにより珠の上，下移動や珠間における吸引現象を防止し，珠の静止を完全にして珠くずれしなよう構成してなるものである。

【語句の説明】

本発明は以上のような欠点を消却してなる：the present invention has overcome the aforementioned problems and disadvantages

マグネチック薄板の吸引力を平均させ：by creating a uniform magnetic attraction throughout the magnetic sheet

上，下移動や珠間における吸引現象を防止し：by preventing the beads from falling down and from sticking to each other.　ここではソロバンを縦に保持して使用することを考えているので，上に移動することはあり得ないので「上，移動」を省略して，訳文は preventing 〜 from falling down としてある。

珠の静止を完全にし：by causing beads to stay at a desired position steadfastly.「完全に」を実際的意味にとり，perfectly とせずに at a desired position steadfastly と

第2章　米国会社の法務部門

している。

【訳　文】

　The present invention has overcome the aforementioned problems and disadvantages. This invention is characterized by preventing the beads from falling down and from sticking to each other by creating a uniform magnetic attraction throughout the magnetic sheet. Further, the present invention is characterized by causing beads to stay at a desired position steadfastly and preventing the beads from being disorderly positioned.

---

④　図面の説明

【例　文】

　図面は本発明の実施例を示すもので第1図はその平面図，第2図は第1図のA-A線断面図，第3図は従来使用されているマグネチック薄板の平面図，第4図は本発明に係るマグネチック薄板の平面図，第5図は珠摺動棒の挿嵌状態を示す正面図，第6図は盲人用ソロバンに使用する珠を示す斜面図である。

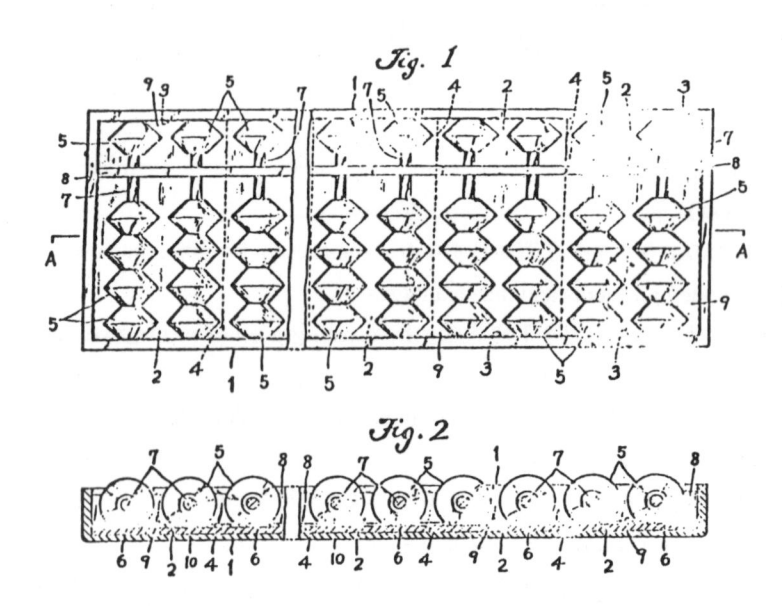

第2節 特許と英語

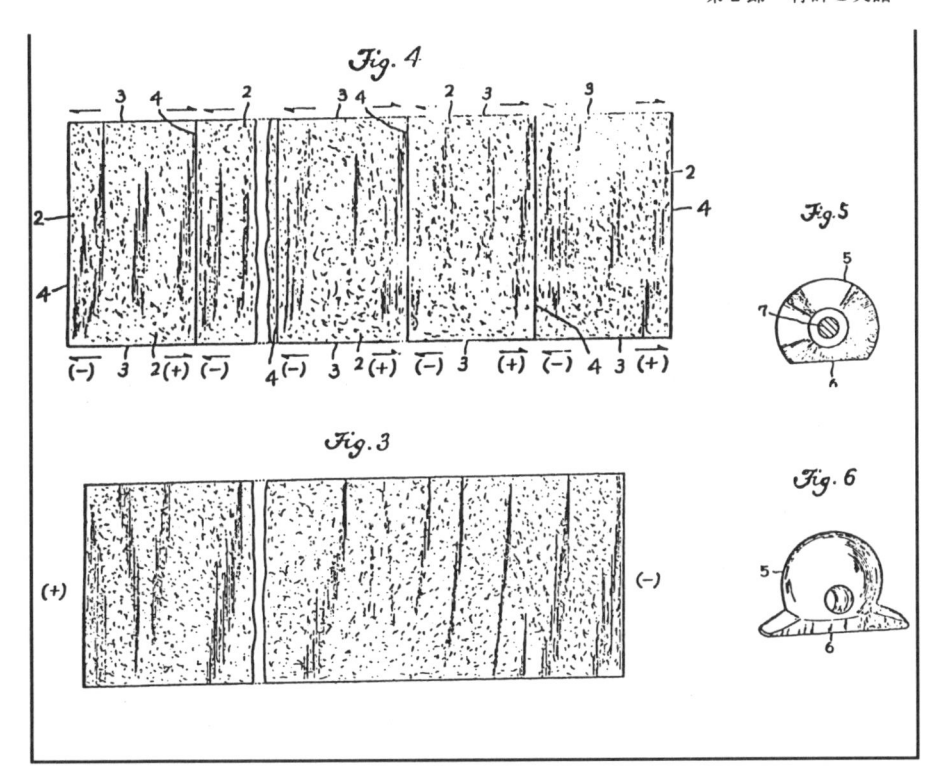

【語句の説明】

図面は本発明の実施例を示す：the drawings show the preferred embodiment of the present invention；英文では preferred が加えられている。

第1図はその平面図：FIGURE 1 is a plan view thereof. 平面図は plane view でなく plan view を使用する。

第2図は第1図のA−A線断面図：FIGURE 2 is a view in section taken as indicated along line A-A in FIGURE 1.

第3図は従来使用されているマグネチック薄板の平面図：FIGURE 3 is a plan view of the magnetic sheet which has been previously used.

第4図は本発明に係るマグネチック薄板の平面図：FIGURE 4 is a plan view of the magnetic sheet of the present invention.

第5図は珠褶動棒の挿嵌状態を示す正面図：FIGURE 5 is a view in side elevation of the bead-travelling road passing through the bead.；elevation とは、あるがままの

53

第2章　米国会社の法務部門

状態を示す言葉。

〜に使用する珠を示す斜面図：a view in perspective of the bead of the soroban for use of 〜

【訳　文】

　The drawings show the preferred embodiment of the present invention. FIGURE I is a plan view thereof. FIGURE 2 is a view in section taken as indicated along line A-A in FIGURE 1. FIGURE 3 is a plan view of the magnetic sheet which has been previously used. FIGURE 4 is a plan view of the magnetic sheet of the present invention. FIGURE 5 is a view in side elevation of the bead-travelling road passing through the bead. FIGURE 6 is a view in perspective of the bead of the soroban for use of the blind person.

---

⑤　先行技術

【例　文】

　つぎに作用効果について説明をすれば，従来は第3図示の如く1枚のマグネチック薄板を横長にして使用するためその両端における吸引力が強く中間部における吸引力が弱くなる欠点があり，珠の静止位置がずれたりして計算が不明確になる欠点があった。

【語句の説明】

つぎに〜について説明をする：Then, an explanation shall be made as to 〜
作用効果について：the function and effect
その両端における吸引力が強く：magnetic attraction is strong at both ends
中間部における吸引力が弱く：weak in the middle part thereof
欠点があり：has the disadvantage
珠の静止位置がずれたりして：The beads in the middle have occasionally slipped out of the proper positions, in the middleと言う語句を補足している。
計算が不明確になる：「正確な計算が不可能になる。」と言い替えて，This has made it impossible to make an accurate calculation or computation.としてある。

第 2 節　特許と英語

【訳　文】

　Then, an explanation shall be made as to the function and effect. As shown in FIGURE 3, a single piece of magnetic sheet has been used in prior art devices. Such device has the disadvantage that magnetic attraction is strong at both ends and weak in the middle part thereof. The beads in the middle have occasionally slipped out of the proper positions. This has made it impossible to make an accurate calculation or computation.

---

⑥　作用効果

【例　文】

　本発明によれば第4図のごとく短辺部3を珠褶動巾の略々2倍巾に形成した複数の長方形状のマグネチック薄板2をその長辺部を縦方向に当接して配設したため磁性は矢印のごとく従来と異なり珠の褶動方向と直角になるため珠が磁性によって上，下移動することもなく珠間における吸引現象も珠褶動棒により解消され珠の上，下移動に影響を与えず磁性が平均しているので整然として珠の上，下および静止が可能であり珠崩れしないソロバンを提供することができる。
　第6図は盲人用ソロバンとして使用する場合の珠を示し，上面に丸みをもたせたもので珠の形状を変えるだけで珠崩れがせず盲人に最適のソロバンを提供することができる。

【語句の説明】

珠褶動巾の略々2倍巾：「褶動」は特に意味がないので省略し，approximately twice as wide as the beads とする。

複数の長方形状のマグネチック薄板2：a plurality of rectangular magnetic sheets 2

その長辺部を縦方向に当接して配設し：the longer sides～are placed so as to be kept in touch with each other lengthways

従来と異なり：～different from prior art devices

珠の褶動方向と直角になる：意訳して「each longer end of each sheet is a pole」とすることにより実質的に同一内容を表現している。

珠が上，下移動する：意訳して beads will not fall downwardly として upwardly は省

55

第 2 章　米国会社の法務部門

略してある。

磁性が平均：the magnetic forces are made uniform

整然として珠の上，下および静止が可能：possible to move the beads up and down regularly, or cause beads to stay at a proper place steadily

盲人用として使用する：for use by blind persons

上面に丸みをもたせた：the upper part 〜 is made roundish

珠崩れがせず：are not made to be disorderly positioned

【訳　文】

　The soroban constructed in accordance with the present invention comprises, as shown in FIGURE 4, a plurality of rectangular magnetic sheets 2 the shorter sides 3 of which are approximately twice as wide as the beads and the longer sides of which are placed so as to be kept in touch with each other lengthways and at which polarities are established.

　Accordingly, the soroban of the present invention is different from prior art devices in that each longer end of each sheet is a pole, and the magnetic forces are therefore made uniform. Therefore, beads will not fall downwardly. Bead-travelling rods prevent the beads from being attracted to each other. The up and down travel of beads is not subject to magnetism. The magnetic attraction is made uniform. Thus, it is possible to move the beads up and down regularly, or cause beads to stay at a proper place steadily.

　FIGURE 6 shows the beads of the soroban which is for use by blind persons. The upper part of the bead is made roundish. It is possible to provide a soroban the beads of which are not made to be disorderly positioned for the use of the blind persons by changing the shape of the bead.

ｂ．英文和訳

①　特許請求範囲の一部

【例　文】

　What I claim is:

1. A magnetic Soroban comprising a rectangular tray; a plurality of rectangular

magnetic sheets on said tray; a magnetically permeable film on said sheets; a beam positioned on said tray parallel to the longer sides thereof; a plurality of bead-travelling rods positioned over said tray perpendicular to said beam; and a desired number of beads sensitive to magnetism positioned on each of said rods for movement there along; whereby the shorter sides of said sheets are approximately twice as wide as said beads and the longer sides of said sheets are positioned in contact with each other and have polarities established thereat.

2. The magnetic soroban according to claim I wherein the width of said shorter sides of said sheets are slightly less than twice the width of said beads.

【語句の説明】

What I claim is：日本特許の「特許請求の範囲」に相当する；これを直訳すれば scope of claim for patent, 発明者が二人以上なら what we claim is とする。

a plurality of rectangular magnetic sheets：複数の長方形状のマグネチック薄板

a magnetically permeable film：磁透性の薄板

parallel to the longer sides thereof：その長辺部に対し平行に

perpendicular to said beam：該梁体に対し垂直に

beads sensitive to magnetism：磁石に対して吸着性を有する珠

approximately twice as wide as said beads：該珠の略々2倍の巾にして

【訳　文】

特許請求の範囲

1．横長浅底の箱体，該箱上体に複数の長方形状のマグネチック薄板，該薄板上の複数の透磁性の薄板，該箱体上に磁透性の薄板，該箱体上にその長辺部に対し平行に位置づけられる梁板，該箱体上に該梁体に対し垂直に位置づけられる複数の珠褶動棒およびそれに沿って運動するべく該珠の各々に位置づけられ磁石に対して吸着性を有する適数の珠よりなり，さらに該薄板の短辺部が該珠の略々2倍の巾にして，該薄板の長辺部は互いに接触するように位置づけられ，かつそこに極性の設けられていることよりなるマグネチックソロバン。

2．該薄板の該短辺部の巾が該珠の巾よりわずかに狭い特許請求範囲1による

第2章　米国会社の法務部門

マグネチックソロバン。

② 書誌的事項

【例　文】

3,508,348
MAGNETIC SOROBAN (ABACUS)

＿＿＿＿＿, 9 ＿＿＿-cho, Shinjuku-ku,
Tokyo, Japan
Filed Nov.28, 1967, Ser.No.686,016
Int. Cl. G06c 1/00
U.S.Cl.35–33　　8 Claims

References Cited
UNITED STATES PATENTS

2,654,164　10/1953　　Seidenberg -------------- 35–33
2,857,686　10/1958　　Blake ------------------- 35–33
2,872,742　2/1959　　Schott ------------------ 35–33

EUGENE R. CAPOZIO, Primary Examiner
W. H. GRIEB, Assistant Examiner

【訳　文】

特許番号：第3,503,343号
磁器ソロバン

発　明　者：（省略）
住　　　所：日本国東京都新宿区＿＿＿＿町9番地
出　願　日：1967年11月28日
出　願　番　号：第686,016号
クレーム数：8
米国分類番号：35–33

58

本特許のファイル中の引例文献
米国特許庁

特許番号第2,654,164；特許月10/1953	発明者；サイデンベルグ	分類；35-33
特許番号第2,857,164；特許月10/1958	発明者；ブレーク	分類；35-33
特許番号第2,872,742；特許月2/1959	発明者；ショット	分類；35-33

　主席審査官：ユウジンR.カポジオ
　審 査 官 補：W.H.グリーブ

c）特許の文法と長いセンテンスの英訳法
(1) 化学特許明細書における動詞のテンス
　a．英文法と実用英語
　筆者の持論は，英語ついてはあまり難しく考えず，「英文法」の勉強も程々にしようと言うことである。しかし，特許のような利害を伴う案件に関しては，やはり英文法の知識も大切である。と言っても，学校英文法で勉強するような難しい「英文法の理論」ではなく，理論的には極めて初歩の英文法の課題である。それは，ある一定の場合に英文の動詞のテンスを「現在形」にするべきか，「過去形」にするべきかの選択の問題で，非常に簡単なことではあるが，特許の命運を左右するほど重要な場合がある。
　b．米国特許明細書中での動詞のテンス
　以下で示すのは，筆者がサラリーマン時代に社内講習の講師として，特許明細書の英訳について話したことをまとめたものである。この文章は，英文法的には極めて初歩の問題であり，受験勉強の対象にもならないであろう。しかし，実務英語の世界では非常に重要である。日本語で化学関係の特許明細書を書くときには，実施例を現在形で書くのか，過去形で書くのかは特別意識しないと思われる。しかし，それを英訳する場合には慎重に考える必要がある。そこで，発明者に「その実施例は，実際に実験をやってみたのですか？，それともデスクワークで仕上げたのですか？」と質問し，確認の上しかるべきテンスの英文を作成しなければならないのである。その理由は，動詞のテンスの如何により，当該特許の命運が左右されるからである。

第2章 米国会社の法務部門

c．学校英文法と異なる語法の支配する業界

米国の化学特許に関して，英文法の常識に反する慣例が支配している。詳細は，以下の説明に譲るが，それは「普遍的な真理については，現在形で表現する。」という英文法の原則と相反する語法である。すなわち，デスクワークで作成され，現実に試験されていない実施例は，現在形で表現すべしと言うことである。

〈米国特許明細書中の動詞のテンス（時制）〉

① 序

化学に関する米国特許明細書をいろいろと読んでいて気が付くことは，文の動詞のテンスが「現在」であったり「過去」であったり，統一されていないことである。

これに対する素朴な疑問は，明細書の英文は現在形でも過去形でもよいのか，また，現在形，過去形にするのは特別の理由があるのかということであった。例えば，十ある明細書の実施例うち三つが現在形の形で記載されていながら，同じ明細書中の他の七つの実施例が過去形の形で記載されていたりすることである。そうすると，いやしくも特許権という権利に係る明細書の作製者が同じ明細書の中で，一部の実施例の記載を現在形で表現しながら，他の実施例を過去形で表現したり，勝手な書き方をするとは考えらなかった。それで，何か特別な理由があってそのような書き方をしているのではないかと，疑問に思っていたところ，最近になってこの疑問に対する解答らしきものを見つけたのでここで紹介する。

② 一つの解決案—英文法の理論

前述の現在形，過去形に関する問題を文法的な面から考察してみる。

動詞の時制のうちの Present tense の用法の一つは，「常に，かつ必然的に真実なもの (what is always and necessarily true)」を表わすためである。例えば，

    The sun shines by day and the moon by night.

    Things equal to the same thing are equal to one another.[1,2]

さらに Louis T. Fieser 氏は，その著書 Style Guide for Chemists[3]（日本語版 18～19

---

1) J.C. Nesfield, English Grammer Series IV, 177 (1901), The Seito-Shobo, 翻刻版：Nesfield. 以下，Nesfield と略す。
2) Yonezo Nitsu, A handbook of English Grammer, 150-151 (1948), The Hokuseido Press.
3) Louis T. Fieser, style guide for Chemists（日本語訳書：T. Goto, S. Yamada）, 18-19 (1966).

第2節　特許と英語

ページ)の中で,「科学的事実は,観測した時がどんなに古くても常に真実であるので,そのことを書くときは現在形を用いる。

    Pasteur discovered that sodium ammonium
    racemate crystallized in two hemihedral forms.

と書くのは間違いであり,それはパスツール(Pasteur)の発見が1848年に一度だけ起こった偶然の現象ではなく,一世紀以上の昔も,また今も正しい科学的事実であるからにほかならない。前文を訂正すると,

    Pasteur discovered that sodium ammonium
    tartrate crystallizes ………

となる。」と書いている。

　このことから,真実なものは常に現在形を用いて表現し,時制の呼応(sequence of tense)の例外をなし,主文が過去形で表現されていても,従文が過去形をとらずに現在形で表現されている。例えば,

    The students were taught that the earth moves round the sun.[4]

　上述の説明から,一般論として現在形と過去形のどちらの時制を用いて文を書くべきかは理解できると思う。すなわち,ある事実が科学的事実ないしは真理である場合には現在形で表現し,そのある事実が,特に実験操作が巧みなためとか,偶然の幸運とかによってもたらされた時は過去形で表現すべきものと考えられる。なお,この事実が普遍的な真理であるか,また偶然的事実であるかの判断は文を書くものの主観的判断によるものとされるであろう。

　そこで,発明者あるいは明細書の作成者が,従文中の事実を真理と考えたために主文と従文との「時制の呼応」の原則を無視して,主文の時制を過去形としながら,従文は現在形を用いている例を実際の米国特許明細書中より引用して次に示す。

    U.S. Patent 2, 895, 977
      (Column 1, lines 47-48)
    It has now been discovered that alkyltrifluorosilanes can be prepared in high yield free from further alkylated silane ………
    U.S. Patent 2, 206, 634
      (Column 1, lines 15-Column 2, line 1)

---

[4] Nesfield, 189-190.

第2章　米国会社の法務部門

　　　We have now discovered that effort in this direction is sound only when
　　　charged particles are used…

　上述の英文法の理論により，現在形にするか過去形にするかの問題は，一応明細書中の実施例以外の一般的記載に関しては解決したように見えるが，実施例の記載の部分は，上述の英文法の理論による説明では解決されないと思う。すなわち，同じ明細書中においてさえも，一部の実施例を現在形の時制を用いて記述しながら，別の実施例には過去形を用いているような，一貫していない場合が往々にあるからである。このことを説明するために，上述の英文法の理論により現在形の実施例は，発明者が一般的科学的事実ないし真理として自信のあるものに関してであり，過去形のものはそれほど自信のあるものでなく，偶然旨くいった実験の報告くらいに考えればよいとの理屈も成立する。しかし，これは一般の文献については妥当するかも知れないが，特許明細書中の実施例に関しては，この説明は適切ではないと思われる。すなわち，実施例は当該発明の好ましき具体例(Preferred embodiment)を示すのが通例であり，また実施例の数が多いからといって，特許発明の保護範囲がそれだけ広くなるものでもないので，あまり自信のない実験の結果を過去形で記載された実施例の形で明細書中に挿入することもあり得ないから，過去形の時制で表現された実施例には，patent practice上，なんらかの特殊の理由が存在するはずである。

③　異なる観点からの解決案
【proposal(提案)説】
　表題のいわゆるproposal(提案)説の前提として，米国特許法上の発明の完成について若干述べる。米国特許法は先発明主義をとっており，中でも，その発明の完成についてconception, diligence, reduction to practiceは重要な観念であるが，その発明の先順位を決定する重要な要素は，発明の着想の日と具現化[注1]の日(The date of conception and reduction to practice)である。

注1) reduction to practiceという語を「実施に移す」などと訳されているが[5]，「実施」という語を使うと，わが国特許法第2条第3項の「実施」と観念的混同を生ずるおそれがあり好ましくないし，またreduction to practiceの意味は

---

5) 訳註外国特許法, 107 (1962).

「The act of embodying an invention in actual physical form」ということなので，「具象化」と訳して使うことにする。

単に着想しただけで，具象化されなければ発明は完成したと言えないからである。
さらに，この具象化は現実的具象化(actual reduction to practice)と法定具象化(constructive reduction to practice)とに分けられ，後者は特許出願により現実の具象化と同様に法律上取扱われることを意味する。

The legal equivalent of an actual reduction to practice is obtained by filing a patent application.[6],[7]

余談になるが，発明の先順位の争いに関する抵触審査手続きについて，米国のpatent attorneyは，先発明者よりは先願の発明者の代理人になるのを好むそうである。この理由は，後願の先発明者はいろいろとconception, reduction to practice等に関する証拠を集めなければならず，争いに勝つのがむずかしいのに反し，先願の出願人の場合はには，たとえ後発明者であっても，その特許出願日およびその明細書の内容だけを根拠として，他の証拠を提出しなくても争いに勝てる可能性が大きくようだ。しかも，その明細書の内容の開示自体が，その出願日現在において発明が完成しているという強い証拠となり，代理人としては容易な事件であるからである。米国の特許制度は，建前として先発明主義を根拠としているといわれながら，現実には「先願保護主義」が支配しているように思われる。

上述の法定具象化(constructive reduction to practice)の制度は，出願人にとってまことに都合のよい制度であるが，化学特許の場合に，実際に試験していない事項，いわゆるデスク・ワークででっちあげた実施例を，米国特許法第112条の「……明細書には発明……実施できるように充分に明瞭，簡潔かつ適正な(exact)語句……」の規定からみて，挿入することができるかどうか問題となるかもしれないと考えられる。

さらに，米国特許庁では，原明細書に記載された事項および特許出願手続の過程において申立てられた事項を，それが偽りのないものであるかどうかを確定するた

---

[6] Howard I.Forman, Patents, Research and Management, 221 (1961), Central Book Company, Inc.
[7] Howard I.Forman, The Law of Chemical, Metallurgical and Pharmaceutical Patente, 263 (1967), Central Book Company, Inc. 以下，L.C.M.P.P.と略す。

第2章　米国会社の法務部門

めに調査する傾向が最近強くなってきており，しかも，明細書中の技術内容の開示が，充分で明瞭，簡潔かつ適正[注2]でなければならないということは，それが発明者の知っている限り，その記載されていることが真実でなければならないということである。

注2）訳註外国特許法[8]では，米国特許法第112条を「明細書には……充分に明瞭，簡潔かつ適切な……語句」と訳されているが，この「適切な」の原語は「exact」であり，このexactの意味が，Webster's Third New International Dictionaryにより「exhibiting or characterized by strict, particular, and complete accordance with fact, truth, or an established standard or original」と説明されていて，「真実と合致せる」というニュアンスがあるので，一応「適正」と訳してみた。

だが，このような考え方に対して，現実に試験していない実施例－すなわち，デスク・ワークでつくりあげた実施例－を明細書中に挿入することは許されるとの考え方である。

1952年の米国特許法は，実施可能な発明の具体例で試験して成功することによって現実的具象化(actual reduction to practice)をはかることよりは，むしろ特許出願をすることによって法定具象化(constructive reduction to practice)をはかる権利を発明者に対して大幅に認めた。それにもかかわらず，もし発明者に対して化学事件の場合に，現実に試験していない事項に関する実施例を明細書中に開示する権利を認めなければ，この法定具象化をはかる権利を保持することができないし，またその意味がないことになってしまう。だから，現実に試験してみない事項に関する実施例を一つ，時によっては多数の実施例を挿入することは全く適切なものであり，また当然なことである。このように，現実に試験をしてみない事項を実施例として明細書に記載することは許されるのであるが，次に考えなければならないことは，現実に試験した事項に関する実施例とそうでない実施例とを同じ態様で表現すればよいのか，あるいは異なった態様で表現すべきかということである。

ここで初めて，実施例が現在形で書かれている場合と，過去形で書かれている場合の相違について述べることになる。

H.I. Forman博士編集の「The Law of Chemical, Metallurgical and Pharmaceutical

---

8) 訳註外国特許法, 107 (1962).

Patents[9]」中には，この問題について次のようにふれている。

「……しかしながら，このようなタイプの現実に試験していない事項に関する実施例の記載にあたっては，その実施例が現実に試験された事項に関する実施例のように記載してはならなず，その実施例は，むしろ一種の提案(proposal)のように記載すべきであると信じている人が多い。そこで，出願の一部には，現実に試験してみた事項に関する実施例を「過去の時制」("reagent A was reacted with reagent B")で記載し，現実に試験してみない事項に関する実施例は，「現在の時制」で記載している」とのことである。

"Many people believe, however, that in stating examples of this type, it should not be stated that the example has been actually worked, but the example should be stated more like a proposal. Thus, some applicants state actually worked examples in the past tense ("reagent A was reacted with reagent B"), and state non-worked examples in the present tense."

④ 実際の米国特許明細書に即しての考察

U.S.Patent 3,211,781 をみてみると，実施例の部分は次のとおりである。

>3,211,781
>PRODUCTION OF E-AMINOCAPROIC ACID
>ESTERS FROM E-AMINOCAPROLACTAM
>Bernard Taub, Williamsvilic, and John B. Hino, Buffalo,
>N.Y., assignors to Ailied Chemical Corporation, New York, N.Y., a corporation
> of New York
>No Drawing. Filed Oct. 28, 1960, Ser. No.65, 614
>5 Claims. (Cl.260-482)

Example 1

A mixture of 56.5 parts of E-caprolactam, 9 parts of water and 52 parts of n-butyl alcohol was heated under reflux for 6 hours white passing a steady stream of hydrogen chloride through the boiling mass. At the end of this time, the hydrogen chloride addition was terminated, and 45 parts of toluene were added to the reaction

---
9) L.C.M.P.P., 291-292.

mixture. The mixture was then refluxed for about 16 hours,during which period water was separated from the condensate prior to returning it to the boiling mass. There after, the mass was distilled under reduced pressure to remove toluene and the excess butyl alcohol. The residue of solid butyl-E-aminocaproate hydrochloride was washed with Skelly B (a mixture of petroleum hydrocarbons boiling in the pentane range), and then dried in a vacuum dessicator. The dried product weighed 110 parts, which is equivalent to a yield of 98.5 % of theory.

Example 2

Following the procedure described in Example 1 above using 91.0 parts of 2-etbylhexanol in place of 52.0 parts of n-butyl alcohol,there was obtained 110 parts of 2-ethylhexyl-E-aminocaproate hydrochloside, as a semisolid which did not crystallize readily. This amount of product is equivalent to 79 % of the theoretical yield.

Example 3

In an analogous manner to that described in Example 2 above,from 91.0 parts of n-octyl alcuhol, there was obtained 130 parts (94 % yield) of n-octyl-E-aminocaproate hydrochloride.

Example 4

By substituting 70.0 parts of cyclohexanol for 52.0 parts of n-butyl alcohol in the process described in Example 1 above, 105 parts, or 85 % of theory, of cyclohexyl-E-aminocaproate hydrochloride were obtained.

Example 5

In a similar manner to that described in Example 1, except that 110.6 parts of n-decyl alcohol were used instead of n-butyl alcobol,there were obtained 141 part (92 % yield) of n-decyl-E-aminocaproate hydrochloride.

Example 6

The procedure of Example 1 was repeated using 130.0 parts of lauryl alcohol in place of butyl alcohol.THe yield of lauryl-E-aminocaproate hydrochloride was 131 parts or 78 % of theoretical yield.

Example 7

By substituting 75.6 parts of benzyl alcohol for 52.0 parts of n-butyl alcohol in the process described in Example 1 above, benzyl-E-aminocaproate hydrochloride is obtained.

Example 8

By substituting 15.5 parts of ethylene glycol for 52.0 parts of n-butyl alcohol in the process described in Example 1 above, ethylene bis-E-aminocaproate hydrochloride is obtained.

Example 9

In a similar manner to that described in Example 1, except that 42.5 parts of pyrrolidone are used in place of E-caprolactam, n-butyl γ-aminobutyrate hydrochloride is obtained.

実施例1から6までは「過去の時制」で書かれており、実施例7から9までは「現在の時制」で書かれている。上述3の提案(proposal)説によると、実施例1から6までは現実に試験してみた実施例であり、実施例7の場合、実施例1の52.0 parts of n-butyl alcoholの代わりに75.6 parts of benzyl alcoholを、また実施例8の場合は、実施例1の52.0 parts of n-butyl alcoholの代わりに15.5 parts of ethylene glycolを用いて、それぞれ、机上の計算により実施例を作成したと考えられる。また実施例9の場合は、実施例1と同様の方法で、E-caprolactumの代わりに42.5 parts of pyrolidoneを用いて、やはり机上の計算で実施例をつくったと推定される。

次に、米国特許明細書のどの位の割合が、現在形と過去形とを区別して実施例の記載をしているかを知りたいと思い、偶然手もとにあった明細書を読んで参考までに次のような表をつくってみた。

U.S. Patent と動詞の時制の対照表

時制 U.S.Patent Number	現在	過去	その他
U.S.P.2,119,741	Ex.1 ~ 4		
U.S.P.2,591,573		Ex.A ~ C	
U.S.P.2,890,985	Ex.A ~ C		Ex1 ~ IV (may be used)
U.S.P.2,895,977		Ex.1	
U.S.P.2,910,480		Ex.1 ~ 20	
U.S.P.2,942,032	Ex.2 ~ 6	Ex.1	
U.S.P.2,963,453	Ex.1 ~ 20		
U.S.P.3,078,228	Ex.1 ~ 29		
U.S.P.3,128,316		Ex.1 ~ 7	

第2章　米国会社の法務部門

　上述のわずか9件のU.S.P.から結論を出すのは早計であるのは当然のことであり，また選択が当を得ているかどうかも疑問であるが，現在形と過去形と分けて実施例を書いているのはU.S.P.2,942,032だけであり，過去形だけで表現したものが4件，現在形だけで表現したものが，やはり4件あり，それぞれ同数である。また，U.S.P.2,890,985のようにexample A～Cが現在形で表現され，example I～IVが「may be used」という動詞の形態をとっている。多分，一方のexamplesは参考例なのであろう。

　過去形だけの実施例が記載されている明細書は，現実に試験した事項についての実施例だけを記載したと推定されるが，もちろんそうでないかもしれない。現在形だけの実施例が記載されている明細書は，その実施例がすべてデスク・ワークで作成されたのか，一部の実施例は，現実に試験した結果によるのかもしれないが，とにかく全部の実施例が提案(proposal)のように記載されていると，後になってから現実に試験していない事実に基づきながら，実際に試験した事実に基づいているような偽りの実施例を記載しているとの非難をうけることはないであろう。

⑤　む　す　び

　米国の特許明細書の動詞のテンスに関する今までの説明から，米国向けの特許明細書を作成する場合の時制の取扱い方に関して，ある程度了解されたことと思う。すなわち，明細書中の一般的記載事項については，上述②の英文法の理論により，また実施例の記載については，上述③の提案(proposal)説にしたがって処理すれば無難であろう。提案(proposal)説は興味ある事実を示している。一つは，米国のpatent practiceでは，デスク・ワークにより作成された実施例の挿入を明細に認めていることであり，他は実施例の記載の時制が現在と過去と区別されている場合には，その区別により，どれが現実の試験に基づいて作成された実施例であり，どれが現実の試験例に基づかないで作成された実施例かが明瞭にわかることは，米国特許明細書を読み，その内容を評価，判断するときの参考となるであろう。

　さらに，提案(proposal)説は，われわれが日本出願に基づいて米国特許出願する際に，作成する英文明細書中のテンスをどのように取り扱うべきかを教えてくれる。すなわち，実施例の作成にあたっては，特定の実施例について，現実に試験がなされたことが確認されている場合以外は，その動詞のテンスを現在形にしておく方が安全であろう。おそらく，実施例が過去形で記載されている特許について，第三者

と特許上の争いが起きた場合は，その特許明細書の過去形で記載された実施例について，現実にはそれがデスク・ワークで作成されたことを証明することに成功した時に，後でその実施例の動詞の時制(テンス)を現在形に訂正することができるか非常に疑問であり，いずれにしても，われわれにとって有利なことはないであろう。したがって，実施例が現実の試験に基づくのか否か明瞭にわからない場合には，英文で表現する際，「現在の時制」を用いるのが賢明である。

(2) 法律の条文，特許のクレームなど

　最近は，極端に長いセンテンスからなる文章は少なくなってきたようである。一時，翻訳の仕事をしていた頃，警察の捜査報告書などの英訳させられた。やたらと長いセンテンスで，しかも難しい言葉が使われていたと記憶する。そのような文章の場合は，できあがった英訳文の読みやすさを考えて，適当に短いセンテンスに分解して訳したものだった。このように，短くすることが許される文章なら問題がないが，どうしても短いセンテンスに分解することの許されないものがある。具体的には，法律の条文と特許などのクレーム(請求範囲)であろう。その中でも税金関係の法律，例えば租税特別措置法やその他種々の行政法規に見られる。また，特許関係書類の中核をなす明細書中の「請求範囲」は1項で記載するのがルールである。細かい技術内容を1項目の英語で記載するとなると，その英文は極めて長いセンテンスになる。また，請求範囲に関する記載でなくともセンテンスが長くなることがよくある。さらに，日本語と英語との文章構成上の相違から，訳文の「係り結びの調整」など困難な問題がある。これを少しでも克服しようとして思いついた解決策が，数学の「代入法」の応用である。それは，$a+b$ を X，$b+c$ を Y，$a+c$ を Z などと置き換えて方程式を簡易化し，その方程式を解いた後に置き換えたものを元に戻す方法である。この方法で英訳するときに応用するわけである。

　本節では，技術文の英訳に「代入法」を利用する例を示すが，法律関係の文の場合も全く同じように応用できる。

　そこで，筆者が以前雑誌の連載で書いた中から，8題の例をあげて解説してみる。

第2章　米国会社の法務部門

> 【例題1】
> 　今まで述べた如く，生物学的試験から5％ものヘキサを含むエチレンビスヂチオカルバミン酸マンガンが，安定剤を加えないマンガン塩とまったく同様に有効であることが証明された。

【語句の説明】

今まで述べた如く：As previously mentioned ; As mentioned above, As set forth hereinbefore

生物学的試験：biological test

5％もの：as much as 5％

〜と同様に有効である：as effective as

安定剤を加えないマンガン塩：manganese salt containing therein no stabilizer, unstabilized manganese salt

　次に文の構成についてみてみよう。そのために数学の代入法を利用する。すなわち，5％ものヘキサを含むエチレンビスヂチオカルバミン酸をA，安定剤を加えないマンガン塩をBとすると，問題文は次のようになる。
「今まで述べた如く，生物学的試験からAがBとまったく同様に有効であることが証明された。」これを英訳してみると，

　　As set forth hereinbefore, biological tests have proven that A is quite as effective as B.

次に，AとBの部分をもとに戻すことにより下記のように訳すことができる。

> 【訳例1】
> 　As set forth hereinbefore, biological tests have proven that the manganese ethylene bisdithiocarbamate containing even as much as 5％ hexa is quite as effective as the unstabilized manganese salt.

> 【例題2】
> 　試験中に生ずる発熱量は，試料の温度と浴温との差を記録する温度差記録装置により記録する。

【語句の説明】
試験中に生ずる～： which develops during the test
発熱量： heating value, exotherm
温度差記録装置： differential recorder
試料の温度と浴温との差： difference between the temperature of the sample and the temperature of the bath

「試験中に生ずる発熱量」をC,「試料の温度と浴温との差」をDとすると，問題文は，「CはDを記録する温度差記録装置により記録する。」となる。この訳文を作ってみると，

　　　C is recorded on a differential recorder which records D.
となる。
　次に，CおよびDの部分をもとにもどし，訳文を作ってみると次のようになる。

---【訳例2】---

　Any exotherm which develops during the test is recorded on a differential recorder which records the difference between the temperature of the sample and the temperature of the bath.

---【例題3】---

　本発明はたとえばラッカー，ペイントの如き油系に顔料を分散または懸濁するに異常に有効な分散剤たる共重合体の製造に関するものである。

これも，「たとえばラッカー，ペイントの如き油系」をEとすると，次のようになる。
　「本発明はEに顔料を分散または懸濁するに異常に有効な分散剤たる共重合体の製造に関するものである。」

【語句の説明】
分散する： disperse
懸濁する： suspend
異常に：本文の意味から判断して **abnormally** などとせずに **exceedingly**, あるいは

exceptionally とする。

有効な分散剤：effective dispensation

共重合体：copolymers

〜するに異常に有効な分散剤：これを「〜するために異常に有効な分散剤」と解し，exceedingly effective dispersants for 〜

本文を次のように英訳する。

> The present invention is concerned with a method for preparing copolymers which are exceedingly effective dispensation for dispersing or suspending pigments in E.

次にEとした部分の英訳をする。

> an oil system such as, for example, lacquer and paint.

以上の説明にしたがい英訳すると次のようになる。

【訳例3】

The present invention is concerned with a method for preparing copolymers which are exceedingly effective dispensation for dispersing or suspending pigments in an oil system such as, for example, lacquer and paint.

【例題4】

該共重合体はN-ビニル2-ピロリドンおよび1種，あるいはそれ以上の油溶性アクリル酸エステル，あるいはメタクリル酸エステルよりなる構造単位を有し，N-ビニルピロリジノンよりの単位は共重合体に約5〜30（重量）%含まれてる。

【語句の説明】

該共重合体：The said copolymer the copolymer

N-ビニル2-ピロリドン：N-vinyl 2-pyrrolidone

1種あるいはそれ以上の：one or more kinds

油溶性アクリル酸エステルあるいはメタクリル酸エステル：oil soluble esters of acrylic or methacrylic acid

N-ビニルピロリジノン：N-vinyl pyrrolidone

第2節　特許と英語

まず「該共重合体は……よりなる構造単位を有し」までの部分の構成方法を研究してみよう。

「N-ビニル-2-ピロリドン」の部分をFとし,「1種あるいはそれ以上の……メタクリル酸エステル」の部分をGとすると,「該共重合体はFおよびGよりなる構造単位を有し」となる。

後半の「N-ビニルピロリジノン……約5～30(重量)％含まれている」の部分は,「N-ビニルピロリジノン……約5～30(重量)％の量で含まれている。」と解する。

文章を前半と後半の部分に分けて二つのセンテンスにすると,英文は次のような構成になる。

The unit form the N-vinyl pyrrolidone is contained in an amount of from about 5 to 30 percent by weight in the copolymer.

The said copolymer has a structural unit consisting of F and G. The unit from the N-vinyl pyrrolidone is contained in an amount of from about 5 to 30 percent by weight in the copolymer.

これを前半と後半の部分を分詞構文を用いて一緒にし,一つのセンテンスにすると,

The said copolymer has a structural unit consisting of F and G, the unit from the N-vinyl pyrrolidone being contained in an amount of from about 5 to 30 percent by weight in the copolymer.

この二つの例のうちの一つを選び,FおよびGの部分をもとの原文に戻し英訳すると次のようになる。

──【訳例4】──────────────────────────
The said copolymer has a structural unit consisting of an N-vinyl-2-pyrrolidone and one or more kinds of oil soluble esters of acrylic or methacrylic acid. The unit from the N-vinyl pyrrolidone is an amount of from about 5 to 30 percent by weight in the copolymer.

──【例題5】──────────────────────────
普通,油中で分散性を与える化合物を処理する時,塩基性窒素を含有する共重合体を使用することを要するが,本発明では塩基性を必要としない。

第2章　米国会社の法務部門

【語句の説明】
分散性：dispensancy
分散性を与える化合物：分散性を与えるための化合物と解して，compounds for providing dispersancy
塩基性窒素：basic nitrogen
塩基性窒素を含有する共重合体：copolymers containing basic nitrogen
塩基性：basicity

これは，「普通，油中……化合物を処理する時」の部分を「普通，油中で……化合物を処理される時」と言い換えて，「when compounds for providing dispersancyis usually treated in oils」とするか，「……処理する時」の「時」を「際して」と解し，次のようにしてもよい。
　　　　　Usually in treating compounds for providing dispersancy in oils.
次に，「分散性を与える化合物」をH，「塩基性窒素を含有する共重合体」をIとすると，「普通，油中でHを処理するとき，Iを使用することを要するが，本発明では塩基性を必要としない。」となる。
これを英訳すると，
　　　Usually in treating H in oils,it is required to use I. However, there is required
　　　no basicity in the present invention.
となり，同じようにもとに戻すと次のようになる。

---【訳例5】---

　Usually in treating compounds for providing dispersancy in oils,it is required to use copolymers containing basic nitrogen. However,there is required no basicity in the present invention.

---【例題6】---

　本発明は，N-ビニル-2-ピロリドンまたは低級アルキル置換N-ビニル-2-ピロリドン，および少なくとも1個のアクリル酸エステルROOCC(Rx)＝CH$_2$〔式中Rはアルキル基，Rxは水素原子あるいはメチル基である〕の共重合体で，N-ビニルピロジノンを該共重合体の5～30(重量)％含み，また該共重合体のエステル部分は少なくとも平均8個の炭素原子を有するアルキル基より成り，

かつ液状石油製品への溶解性を付与せしめた共重合体を製造することにある。

【語句の説明】

本発明は～することにある：The present invention resides in ～；あるいは若干融通をきかせて The object of the present invention is to ～ としてもよいと思う。

低級アルキル置換N-ビニル-2-ピロリドン：lower alkyl substituted N-vinyl-2-pyrrolidone

アクリル酸エステル：acrylic ester

式中Rは～である：Wherein R represents ～

～該共重合体の5～30(重量)％含み：containing in amount of 5 to 30 percent (by weight) of said copolymer

エステル部分：ester portion

エステル部分は少なくとも平均8個の炭素原子を有するアルキル基よりなり：the ester portion consisting of an alkyl group or groups having eight carbon atoms on the average.

これは相当に複雑なので、初めに代入法により簡単にした上で英訳文を作り、その後で省略した部分を埋めて訳例を示すことにする。

「N-ビニル-2-ピロリドン」をJ、「低級アルキル置換N-ビニル-2-ピロリドン」をK、「少なくとも1個のアクリル酸エステル……」をL、「該共重合体のエステル部分」をM、「液状石油製品」をNとすると、次のようになる。

「本発明は、JまたはKおよびLの共重合体で、Mを該重合体の5～30(重量)％含み、またNは少なくとも平均8個の炭素原子を有するアルキル基より成り、かつOへの溶解性を付与せしめた共重合体を製造することにある。」

The present invention resides in producing copolymers of J or K and L, containing M in an amount of 5 to 30 percent (by weight) of said copolymers with N consisting of an alkyl group or groups having eight carbon atoms on the average, and having imparted a solubility to O.

さらに、上述の英文のJ、K、L、M、N、Oの部分をもとに戻してから挿入して、訳例を示すことにする。

第2章　米国会社の法務部門

【訳例6】

　The present invention resides in producing copolymers of an N-vinyl-2-pyrrolidone or a lower alkyl substituted N-vinyl-2-pyrrolidone and at least one acrylic ester ROOCC(Rx)=CH₂ (wherein R represents an alkyl group or groups and Rx represents a hydrogen atom or methyl group), containing an N-vinyl pyrrolidone in an amount of 5 to 30 percent (by weight) of said copolymer with the ester portion thereof consisting of an alkyl group or groups having eight carbon atoms on the average, and having imparted a solubility to liquid petroleum products.

【例題7】

　その後乾燥して，もし必要ならば，微粒子に擂り砕く。同様にして，先にできるエチレンビスヂチオカルバミン酸のジナトリウム塩は，それを水に溶解し，マンガン塩の水溶液を溶かしたエチレンビスヂチオカルバミン酸のジナトリウム塩に加えることにより使用することができる。

【語句の説明】

その後：Hereafter, afterwards, subsequently

その後乾燥する：It is subsequently dried；after it is dried

もし必要ならば：if necessary：もし可能ならばif possible；このようなphraseはカンマで括り，文の適当な場所に挿入するのに便利なものである。

微粒子に擂り砕く：「擂り砕く」は，grindと訳す。「微粒子に」は「微粒子の程度までに」と解し，この「程度までに」に該当する語がtoである。すなわち，to fine particle size. 本文の最初のセンテンスは次のように訳してみる。

　　It is subsequently dried and, if necessary, ground to fine particle size.

同様にして：similarly

先にできる……：pre-formed；例えば，「先にできる二硫化炭素」ならばpre-formed carbon disulfideとする。このようにpre-formedという語を用いると簡潔に表現できることがある。

マンガンの水溶液：an aqueous solution of a manganese salt.

第2節　特許と英語

後半の部分を仮りに，最初にできる……ジナトリウム塩をP，マンガンの水溶液をQ，溶かした……ジナトリウム塩をP'とすると，次のように簡単になる。

「同様にして，PはこれをPに溶解し，QをP'に加えることにより使用することができる。」これを英訳すると，

　　　Similarly, P may be employed by dissolving it in water and adding Q to P'

これを戻して書き直してみると次のようになる。

　　　Similarly, pre-formed disodium ethylene bisdithiocarbamate may be employed by dissolving it in water and adding an aqueous solution of a manganese salt to the dissolved disodium ethylene bisdithiocarbamate.

これに前半部分をつないで，次のように英訳してみる。

【訳例7】

　It is subsequently dried and, if necessary, ground to fine particle size. Similarly, preformed disodium ethylene bisdithiocarbamate may be employed by dissolving it in water and adding an aqueous solution of a manganese salt to the dissolved dis odium ethylene bisdithiocarbamate.

【例題8】

　それによると，この方法は水溶液中で苛性ソーダ，エチレンジアミンおよび二硫化炭素を反応させることにより，エチレンジオカルバミン酸のジナトリウム塩をつくることからなるものである。

これも同様に，「その方法は，R中でS，TおよびUを反応させることによりVをつくることからなるものである」というような簡単なもので，これに相当する英文は，

　　　The method comprises the preparation of V by the reaction of S, T and U in R

となる。

これに多少の抜粋がつき，化合物の名称が長くなっているが次のようになる。

【訳例8】

　The method set forth therein comprises the preparation of dis odium ethylene bisdithiocarbamate by the reaction of sodium hydroxide, ethylene diamine and carbon disulfide in aqueous solution.

第2章 米国会社の法務部門

d) その他
(1) 特許を受ける権利の譲渡書

特許出願をすることのできるのは，本来発明者である。しかし，会社など法人が特許出願するためには一定の手続きが必要である。すなわち，会社などはわれわれ自然人のように実体（肉体）を持っているわけではないので，会社が発明をするわけではない。したがって，会社が特許出願をするためには，本来研究をした者（社員）から譲渡書を得なければならない。この譲渡書には，その発明をした者（社員）の氏名，住所，発明の名称，特許を受ける権利を会社またはその承継人に譲渡する旨，その会社の設立の準拠法（すなわち，どこの国の法律により当該会社が設立されたか），どの国で特許を受ける権利を譲渡するのか，たとえば，日本かアメリカなのかなどを記載すべきである。上記の要件を満たす書類は次のようなものである。

Assignment of Invention

I, the undersigned, John Doe, at No.35, 1-chome, Iroha-cho, Nakano-ku, Tokyo, Japan do hereby declare that I am the true inventor of the invention entitled

Fungcidal Composition

and that I have assigned the right of obtaining patent (or registration of utility model) in respect of the invention entitled above, unto Iroha Kogyo K.K., a corporation organized and existing under the laws of Japan, having its place of business at No. 11, 2-chome, Kanda Minami-cho, Chiyoda-ku, Tokyo, Japan, or its successor, so far as the United States of America is concerned.

This 10th day of December, 2000
John Doe （署　名）
John Doe （タイプ）

次に，上述の英文について譲渡書を英文で作成する場合のことを考慮して説明する。

【解　説】

Assignment of Invention：譲渡というと普通はtransferという言葉を使いたくなるが，assignmentというのが譲渡を意味する法律用語であり，この方が適しているようである。○○書とあると窮屈に考えて，必ず「written」という訳をつけ加えたくなるが，この方がすっきりしていてよい思う。たとえば，申請書とか願書という場合に，「written application」としないで，ただ単にapplication」としておく。

John Doe：日本語の法律文書において，人名の例に書く甲野乙太郎に相当する言葉である。米国では，一般的に原告を示す場合にJohn Doeを用い，被告を示す場合にはRichard Roeを用いる。

patent (or registration of utility model)：米国に出願する場合には実用新案制度がないから，registration of utility modelの部分は抹消しておくことにする。しかし，ドイツに出願する場合には，そのままにしておく。当該発明が，ドイツでは特許法により保護されるか，実用新案法により保護されるか不明だからである。

so far as the United States of America is concerned：ドイツで特許を受ける権利を譲渡する場合には，the United States of AmericaをGermanyにすることは言うまでもない。

上述の譲渡書(Assignment of Invention)のアンダーラインを引いた部分は，適当に入れ替えて利用できるよう参考までに引いておいただけである。

(2) 特許譲渡に関する法的根拠

a．特許法第35条(職務発明)と三通りの英訳

日本の特許法においては，会社の社員などが職務発明をした場合には，特許を受ける権利をだれが取得するのか(会社か，社員か)について，その第35条に規定している。ところが，ドイツの特許法にはその規定がなく，単独法をもって定めている。またアメリカにおいては，従業者発明制度を定めている規定がないばかりでなく，その制度を定めている単独法もない。それで，アメリカの場合には従業者発明の取り扱いを法律解釈の問題としないで，原則として使用者と従業者との間の雇用契約の問題として取り扱っている。実際の取り扱いはケース・バイ・ケースで，発

第2章　米国会社の法務部門

明者に1ドルを支払い（有償契約），特許を出願する権利の譲渡を受けるわけである。余談だが，そのため筆者は，譲渡書作成のため1ドル紙幣の札束を持ち，"one-dollar millionaire" などと呼ばれながら研究所まわりをしたものである。

　以下に，特許法第35条（職務発明）に関する規定の一部を紹介し，さらに刊行物に発表されているその英訳例を三通り示す。詳しくは，次項の「(2) 読みやすい英訳文をつくるコツ」で解説する。

【例　文】

特許法　第35条（職務発明）

　使用者，法人，国または地方公共団体（以下「使用者等」という。）は，従業者，法人の役員，国家公務員，または地方公務員（以下「従業員等」という。）がその性質上当該使用者等の業務範囲に属し，かつ，その発明をするに至った行為がその使用者等における従業者等の現在または過去の職務に属する発明（以下「職務発明」という。）について特許を受けたとき，または職務発明について特許を受ける権利を承継した者がその発明について特許を受けたときは，その特許権について通常実施権を有する。

2．従業者等がした発明については，その発明が職務発明である場合を除き，あらかじめ使用者等に特許を受ける権利もしくは特許権を承継させまたは使用者等のため専用実施権を設定することを定めた契約，勤務規則その他の条項は，無効とする……。

　次に，刊行物に発表されている特許法の三種の英訳の中から，上述の紹介部分の訳例を示す。

【訳例 a】

ARTICLE 35

　An employer, a juridical person,the state or a local public entity (hereinafter referred to as "employer, etc.") shall, in case an employee,an officer of juridical person, a national public service personnel or a local public service personnel (hereinafter referred to as "employee, etc.") has obtained a patent on an invention belonging to the scope of business functions of said employer,etc.in its nature, and to the acts leading to such invention in the past or present duty of employee, etc.of such employer, etc. (hereinafter referred to as "invention in service"), or in case person succeeding to the right to obtain a patent with regard to the invention in service, has obtained a patent on such invention, have a non-exclusive license as to such patent right.

2. With regard to an invention made by an employee, etc. the provisions of a contract,regulations of duty or any other stipulation prescribing beforehand to have employer, etc. succeeded to the right to obtain a patent or a patent right or to establish an exclusive license for employer, etc., shall, except for the case where such invention is an invention in service, be null and void.

【訳例 b 】

Article 35. (Invention of Service)

An employer, a juristic person, the state or a local public entity (hereinafter referred to as the "employer etc.") shall, When an employee, an officer of the juristic person, a person in the national public service or a person in the local public service (hereinafter referred to as the "employee etc.") has obtained patent on an invention which, in its nature, belongs within the scope of the business of the employer etc. concerned and which was accomplished through acts which belong to the persent or past duties of the employee etc. with respect to the employer etc. (hereinafter referred to as the "invention in servise") or when a person who has succeeded to the right to obtain patent on an invention in service has obtained patent on such invention, possess an ordinary license with respect to the patent right concerned.

2. As regards an invention accomplished by an employee etc. with the exception of the case where such invention is an invention in service, the provisions of a contract, service regulations or other stipulations by which it is stipulated in advance the employer etc.shall be allowed to succeed to the right to obtain patent or to the patent right or that an exclusive license shall be created on behalf of the employer etc. shall be invalid.

---【訳例 c】--

ARTICLE 35.（Invention of service）

　An employer, a juridical person, a state or a local public entity (hereinafter referred to as the "employer etc.") shall, in case an employee, an executive officer of a juridical person, a national or local public official (hereinafter referred to as the "employee etc.") has obtained a patent for an invention which falls in nature within the business of the employer etc. and the act resulting in this invention belongs to the present or past duties of the employee etc. of the employer etc. (hereinafter referred to as the "invention in service"), or in case the person who has succeeded to the right to obtain a patent for the invention in service has obtained a patent therefor, have a non-exclusive license on the patent right.

　2. As to an invention made by the employee etc., except an invention in service, the provisions of the contract, the service regulations or other stipulations prescribing in advance the succession of the employer etc. to the right to obtain a patent therefor or the patent right or the establishment of an exclusive license for the employer etc. shall be null and void.

---

b．読みやすい英訳文作成のコツ

　上述の職務発明に関する三つの英訳例を利用して「読みやすい英訳文」の書き方を解説してみよう。

　まず，原文の構成について検討してみる。その骨組みは，「使用者は従業者が特許を受けたとき，または承継した者が特許を受けたときは，その特許権について通常実施権を有する」ということである。

　英訳例 a，b および c ともに，日本文に対応する英文の書き出し方はよいと思う。原文では「特許を受けたとき……」とあるが，この「とき」を訳例 a および b のように「in case ……」と訳した方が，法律文書のスタイルから考えて訳例 a のように「when」と訳よりは better であると思う。

　「通常実施権を有する」：この「有する」を訳例 b のように「possess」とするよりは，訳例 a および c のように，have としたほうがやはり法律文の訳としては better であると思う。「通常実施権」は，単純に non-exclusive license と訳す方がよ

いであろう。訳例aおよびcではそのように訳されている。訳例bではordinary licenseと訳されているが、原文の「通常実施権」の「通常」という言葉にとらわれて「ordinary」としなくてもよいと思う。

　また、訳例bではordinary licenseと訳しながら第2項では専用実施権のことをわざわざ「exclusive license」と訳している。無理して、通常実施権を「ordinary license」とするならば、専用実施権を「extraordinary license」とでもしたらどうだろうか。もっとも、専用実施権をextraordinary licenseと訳すことは、その意味内容から判断すると、全くextraordinaryなものであろう。そこで、「通常」の言葉にとらわれずに実施権とは何かを考え、その意味内容を把握してみると、実施権には二つのタイプがあり、それは専用実施権とそうでないもの、すなわち通常実施権であることを理解するであろう。

　次に、専用実施権に相当するexclusive licenseであるが、専用実施権でないもの、すなわち通常実施権を英語でどう表現するかを考えてみる。そうすると、専用実施権でないものをズバリ表す英語の言葉はないが、しかし法律および特許関係の英文を読んでみると、英語を母国語とする人々がそれに相当する観念を伝えるために慣用しているのがnon-exclusive licenseであることに気づくであろう。

　「国家公務員または地方公務員」：これは訳例aおよびbのどちらでもよいと思うが、訳例cのようにa national or local public officialとせずに、a national public official or local public officialのように、省略せずに書くのがよいだろう。

　もっとも、原文が「国家または地方公務員」であるならば、訳例cの訳語でよいであろう。法律の文章は、できるだけ原文に忠実に訳すように努め、意味の通ずる限りでは、できるだけ直訳するように努めるべきものと思う。

　「業務範囲」：訳例aにおいて、なぜthe scope of business functionとしてfunctionという言葉を使ったのか理解しがたい。

　「特許権」：patent right；特許を受ける権利はright to obtain patentで、両者の異なることを理解しておくこと。

　次に、特許法題35条第2項の構文について述べる。この原文は、「従業者等＿＿発明については」と「その発明が＿＿を除き」と「あらかじめ＿＿無効とする」の三つに分けることができる。

　この三つのグループの組み合わせ方を訳例で検討してみると、「その発明が職務

83

発明である場合を除き」の部分が，訳例 a では訳文の後半にきているが，訳例 b および c では訳文の前半にきていることに気が付くであろう。どの訳例が一番よく原文の意味を伝えているか，読者諸氏が研究してみられると面白いと思う。ただ，この場合にはそんなに大きな相違がないと思う。

実際の和文英訳でもっとも大切なことは，大きく分けた原文中の語句のグループを翻訳した後に，これらの語句のグループをどのように組み合わせて文章を作るかと言うことである。この語句のグループの組み合わせ方いかんにより，その訳文の読みやすさが変わってくるのである。

個々の語句については，必ず手許に特定の専門業務に関する辞典類が準備されていると思うので，どういう英語で表現するかはあまり問題ではない。それよりも，10年以上も翻訳者としての経験があり，vocabulary も驚くほど豊富なのに，意味不明な misleading な英文を書いてしまう人がいる。これらの人は，ただ語句の知識を増すことのみに専念して，語句のグループをどのように組み立てればわかりやすく，誤解されることのない明瞭な英文を書けるのかの研究を怠っているからである。

この語句のグループの組み合わせ方のコツを心得ている人は，たとえ英文を作る経験年数が短くても，達意の英文を巧みに書くことを知っている。すなわち，その語句のグループの組み合わせ方を会得するには，英訳文を作った後で，これら語句のグループを英文のいろいろの位置に挿入した上で，その英文を読んでみる。そして，どの位置にどのグループの語句を挿入したときに，もっともよく原文の意味を伝えているかをみることである。現在では，パソコンを利用すればこのようなことは簡単にできるはずである。

(3) 基本的な図面に関する用語

特許に関する文書には図面が添付されることが多々ある。本項では，図面に関する基本用語，数種を紹介する。その説明は，ただ辞書の訳語を羅列することではなく，自然な語句の組み合わせを紹介することである。

【例 文】

1図は本発明の研削，研磨条帯の斜面図，2図はその拡大断面図，3図は他の方法によって製造した研削，研磨条帯の拡大断面図，4図は製造工程を略図的に示す説明図，5図はその要部の拡大断面図，6図は本発明に係る研削，研磨条帯の使用状態を示す斜面図である。

第 2 節　特許と英語

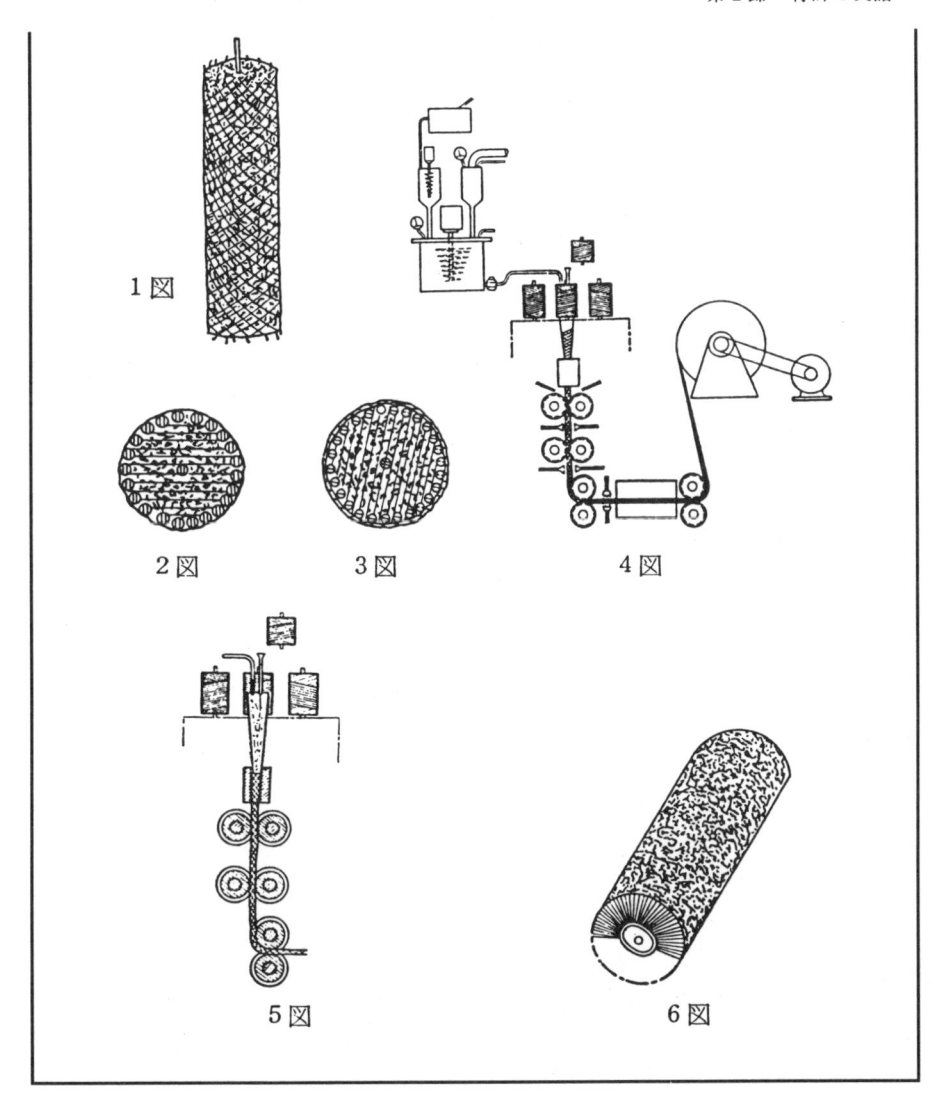

1 図

2 図　　3 図　　4 図

5 図　　6 図

【語句の説明】

斜面図：oblique view figure でよいであろうが，a view in perspective としたほうがよい。

拡大断面図：これも同様に magnified cross view としないで，a magnified view shown in cross section とする。

85

第2章　米国会社の法務部門

他の方法によって製造した研削，研磨条帯の拡大断面図：a magnified view shown in cross section of the grinding and polishing belt prepared in accordance with the different method of this invention.

製造工程を略図的に示す説明図：これを直訳してan explanatory view showing an outline of the manufacturing processと書けなくもないが，少し工夫してみる。そこで「示す」をshowと訳さないで「～を説明する略図的な図」と言い換えて，a diagram illustrating the manufacturing processとすると，より英語らしい表現となる。

要部：essential parts

使用状態を示す：これもこのまま直訳しないで，その意味から「使用状態にある～条帯」と言い換えて，「～the belt which is in use」とする。

以上の説明にしたがい訳例を作る。

【訳　文】

　　Figure 1 is a view in perspective of the grinding and polishing belt of this invention. Figure 2 is a magnified view shown in cross section thereof. Figure 3 is a magnified view shown in cross section of the grinding and polishing belt prepared in accordance with the different method of this invention. Figure 4 is a diagram illustrating the manufacturing process. Figure 5 is a magnified view in cross section of the essential parts thereof. Figure 6 is a view in perspective of the grinding and polishing belt of the present invention which is in use.

このように，刊行物に発表されている英訳例をみると，和文英訳の解答は数学のそれと異なり，ただ一つでないことが理解されたであろう。英訳の参考書をみて，その模範となる英訳文を覚えただけでは不充分であって，各自でいろいろと訳し方を研究してみなければならない。

第3章　特約店・代理店契約

　今や様々な商品が街に溢れ，欲しい物は何でも手に入る世の中になってきたのだが，よく商品を手に取ってその裏を見ると，ほとんどの商品に「製造元」，「発売元」，「販売代理店」等の表示を見かける。もちろん，製造元直売，産地直売もあるが，全体から見ると製造・生産者と発売・販売者は別になっている。このように，商品の流通にはいくつかの企業が介在することにより，消費者の元へ届けられているわけである。すなわち，商品を販売するためには，製造元と販売者との間で契約が交わされて流通されるのである。この販売の形態には，「特約店(Distributor)」と「代理店(Agency)」がある。ただ一般的に，どちらも代理店契約と称しているのだが，正確には上述のようになっている。その契約は，前者が「特約店契約(Distributor agreement)」，後者が「代理店契約(Agency agreement)」である。

　両者の違いは，代理店契約では必ず「手数料(on a commission basis)」の支払い条件が入っているが，特約店はメーカーなどから特定の地域で，特に卸売りのレベルで商品を扱うのを認められている(authorized by a manufacturer or company to market goods especially at wholesale level in a particular area……)者を指している。ただ，これは原則であって，代理店契約書の中には「手数料」の条件が入っていながら，英文のタイトルがDistributor agreementとなっているものもある。様々な国と取り引きする場合は，全てが原則どおりに行われないことが多いので，特に契約の内容に関してはしっかり把握しておくことが重要である。

第3章　特約店・代理店契約

第1節　特約店契約

ここでは，ある特約店契約書の例文をいくつかに分解して説明する。

【例　文】

DISTRIBUTOR AGREEMENT

1. **Parties**：
   a．KO Kabushiki Kaisha（"KO"）：
   Country or state in which organized：Japan
   Address：＿＿＿＿＿＿＿ Minato-ku, Tokyo
   b．Full corporate name or other name of distributor（"Distributor"）：
   ＿＿＿＿＿＿＿＿＿＿＿＿＿＿＿＿＿＿＿＿＿＿＿＿＿＿＿＿＿
   Country or state in which organized：＿＿＿＿＿＿＿＿＿＿＿
   Address：＿＿＿＿＿＿＿＿＿＿＿＿＿＿＿＿＿＿＿＿＿＿＿＿

【語句の説明】

Party：当事者
Kabushiki Kaisha：株式会社；いろいろな訳があるが，一応原文のままとする。
address：住所，所在地
Name：同じnameでも個人なら氏名，法人なら名称とする。
Country of state in which organized：設立された国または州

【訳　文】

特約店契約

1．当事者：
   a．甲株式会社（"甲"）：
   設立準拠法所属国または州：日本
   住所：東京都港区＿＿＿＿＿＿＿＿＿＿＿＿
   b．特約店の正式名称またはその他の名称（「特約店」）：＿＿＿＿＿＿

設立準拠法所属国または州：＿＿＿＿＿＿＿＿＿＿＿＿＿＿
　　　住所：＿＿＿＿＿＿＿＿＿＿＿＿＿＿＿＿＿＿＿＿＿＿＿＿

【例　文】

2. **Effective Date of this Agreement**：＿＿＿＿＿＿＿＿＿＿＿＿＿＿
3. **"KO" Policy**：The policy of "KO" is to select respected and competent distributors who have the ability to sell "KO" products in areas where "KO" determines that sales through distributors are desirable. "KO" supports its distributors by providing such marketing and technical advice, information, literature and other sales assistance as "KO" considers appropriate.
4. **Appointment of Distributor: Non-exclusivity of Appointment**：
    a．"KO" hereby appoints the Distributor as a distributor of those "KO" products listed in Exhibit A (the "KO Products") for the territory described in Exhibit B (the "Territory"). The Distributor hereby accepts such appointment.
    b．The appointment of the Distributor will not preclude "KO" from appointing other distributors for the "KO Products" within the Territory nor will "KO" be prevented from making direct sales of any "KO Products" to customers in the Territory.

【語句の説明】
who have the ability to……：……をする能力
technical advice：技術上のアドバイス
as "KO" considers appropriate：甲が適切と考える
appointment：任命，指名，指定
exhibit：説明用の資料，別表，裁判で提出する証拠
territory：地域，領土，領域
will not preclude from……：が……するのを妨げない
direct sale：直接販売

第3章 特約店・代理店契約

【訳 文】

2．本契約発効日：＿＿＿＿＿＿＿＿

3．甲の方針：甲の方針は甲が販売代理店を通しての販売が望ましいと認める地域において甲の製品を販売する能力を有し，尊敬されかつ有能な特約店を選択することにある。甲は，甲が適切と考えるマーケッティング上もしくは技術上の助言，情報，文献，その他販売に関する助力を提供することによって当該特約店を援助する。

4．特約店の指定・非独占的指定：

a．甲は，「特約店」を本契約により，別表Bに記載した地域(「地域」)における別表Aに記載した製品(「甲製品」)の特約店に指定する。「特約店」は該指定を承諾する。

b．「特約店」の指定は，甲が「該地域」における製品向けに他の特約店を指定するとを妨げるものではなく，また甲が「該地域」において顧客に対し直接製品を販売することを妨げるものでもない。

【例 文】

5. Duties of Distributor：

a．The Distributor will purchase from "KO" and actively promote and resell the "KO Products" in the Territory.

b．The Distributor will provide "KO" with such sales reports and other sales-related information as "KO" may request.

c．At "KO"s request, the Distributor will meet with "KO"s representative at least quarterly to discuss and establish sales targets.

d．The Distributor will use "KO" trademarks on labeling, advertising and sales material. However, the above does not apply where the Distributor is otherwise authorized in writing by "KO". Also, the Distributor will not use any such trademarks for the "KO Products" that are reformulated or otherwise changed by the Distributor.

e．The Distributor will receive "KO" labels for the "KO Products" When it relabels the "KO Products", the Distributor (except for the cases where it reformulates or otherwise changes the "KO Products") will include the

warnings and safe handling and use instructions from the "KO" labels (and any revisions thereto) as part of its own labels for such products.
　　ｆ．The Distributor will comply with all applicable laws in the resale of the "KO Products".
　　ｇ．The Distributor has no authority to act on behalf of "KO".
６．Prices: Conditions of Sale：
　　ａ．The terms and conditions of sale which will apply to all sales to the Distributor will be solely as set forth in Exhibit C unless "KO" otherwise expressly agrees in writing.
　　ｂ．Each order will be subject acceptance by "KO", which has the right to reject any order.

第5項aが特に「『甲製品』を……再販する」の部分が，特約店契約の特徴を示している。

【語句の説明】
promote：普及する，(販売などを)促進する
resell：再販する
"KO" representative：甲の代表者，転じて販売などの担当者，したがって甲の担当者
at least quarterly：少なくとも年4回，年4回以上
trademark：brand nameと同義，trade nameなら商号，場合によっては商品名
applicable laws：適用される法律
have (has) no authority to do……：……をする権限を有しない
as set forth in Exhibit C：別表Cに記載されているように
unless…otherwise…agreed：別段の合意ある場合を除き
subject to acceptance：承諾を条件とする
the right to reject：拒絶する権利

【訳　文】
　５．特約店の義務：
　　ａ．「特約店」は「地域」において甲から「甲製品」を貰い受け，積極的に宣伝し販売を促進し再販する。

b．「特約店」は甲の請求ある場合には，甲に対し販売報告書その他販売に関する情報を提出する。

　　c．甲の請求により，特約店は甲の担当者と販売目標について話し合い，これを設定するために少なくとも年4回の会合をもつ。

　　d．「特約店」はラベル，広告，販売資料に甲の商標を使用する。ただし，「代理店」が書面により甲より別段の許しを受けている場合には別とする。また，「特約店」は再販前に「特約店」が再生，その他の変更を加えた甲の製品について甲の商標を使用しない。

　　e．「特約店」は「甲製品」について甲のラベルを受領する。(再生あるいはその他の変更を加える場合は別として)，特約店がラベルの貼り直しをする場合には，甲のラベルの注意事項，安全な取り扱い方ならびに使用に関する指図(これらの変更を含む)を当該製品用の自己のラベルの中にその一部として記載する。

　　f．「特約店」は甲製品の再販にあたり適用されるすべての法律を遵守する。

　　g．「特約店」は甲に代わって行為をする権限を有しない。

6．価格・販売条件：

　　a．「特約店」に向けのすべての販売に適用される販売条件は，甲が書面により特に同意をした場合を除き，専ら別表Cの記載による。

　　b．個別の注文は甲の承諾を条件とし，甲は注文を拒絶する権限を有する。

【例　文】

7. Confidentiality：

　　a．From time to time "KO" may disclose to Distributor confidential information relating to the "KO Products" ("Confidential Information"). Confidential information shall not include (1) any information which was already in the possession of Distributor, as evidenced by its written records, at the time of the disclosure by "KO", (2) any information which is lawfully received by Distributor from a third party which is not under a secrecy obligation to "KO", and (3) any information which, at the time of disclosure to Distributor or thereafter, becomes public knowledge otherwise than through a breach of Distributor's obligations under this agreement. All

第1節　特約店契約

> disclosures of Confidential information shall be made, or confirmed, in writing and shall be marked "Company Confidential" or with some label indicating their confidentiality.
> b．Distributor agrees not to disclose any Confidential Information to any third party unless such disclosure shall be approved in writing by "KO".
> c．Distributor shall not use any such Confidential Information except as may be necessary or appropriate to carry out its responsibilities under this agreement.
> d．Distributor may disclose Confidential Information to those of its employees who have a need to know such information to carry out the duties of Distributor under this agreement, provided that each such employee.
> 　(1) shall be information of Distributor's responsibility under this agreement with respect to such information, and
> 　(2) shall have agreed in writing to hold confidential, and not disclose or use, any information obtained in the course of his or her employment.
> 　Distributor agrees, upon written request from "KO", to enforce against any such employee, or permit "KO" to enforce against any such employee on Distributor's behalf, employee's obligations of confidentiality.
> e．Any violation by Distributor of its obligations pursuant to this section 7 shall not be adequately compensable by monetary damages and "KO" shall be entitled to an injunction or other appropriate decree specifically enforcing Distributor's obligations pursuant to this section 7.
> f．Distributor's obligations under this section 7 shall survive any termination of this agreement.

【語句の説明】

confidentiality：秘密保持，機密保持
a third party who is not under a secrecy obligation：秘密保持義務を負わない第三者
a breach of ……obligation：……義務の不履行
public knowledge：公知
carry out：実行する，履行する

in the course of one's employment：職務の過程で，職務上，職務に関し
permit KO to enforce…on Distributor's behalf：甲が特約店に代わって……を強制することを認める
pursuant to……：……にしたがって，……によって
adequately：適切に，十分に

【訳　文】

7．秘密保持：
　a．甲は「特約店」に対し，随時「甲製品」に関する秘密情報(「秘密情報」)を開示する。「秘密情報」は以下の情報を含まないものとする。
　　(1) 甲によって開示された時点で，すでに「特約店」の占有下にある文書であることが記録によって証明できる情報
　　(2) 甲に対して秘密保持の義務を有しない第三者から「特約店」が適法に受領した情報
　　(3)「特約店」に対して開示されたとき，またはそれ以降に本契約による「特約店」の義務の不履行によることなく公知となった情報
　　　機密情報の開示はすべて文書によってなされ，または文書により確認され，かつ "Company Confidential" と表示されるかまたは秘密である旨のラベルで表示される。
　b．「特約店」は，甲によって文書をもって許される場合は別として，第三者に対し秘密情報も開示しないことに合意する。
　c．「特約店」は本契約に基づく責務の履行に必要または適切である場合を除き，「秘密情報」を使用しない。
　d．「特約店」は，従業員が本契約に基づく「特約店」の義務を履行するために秘密情報を知る必要がある従業員に対し，「秘密情報」を開示することができる。ただし，以下の場合に限る。
　　(1) 当該各従業員に対し，当該情報に関して本契約上に基づく「特約店」の義務を知らせてある場合
　　(2) 当該各従業員が，職務に関し取得した情報を秘密とし，開示しないことおよび使用しないことを文書によって合意している場合
　　　「特約店」は甲から文書により要求があった場合，該従業員に対して，従業員の秘密保持義務を強制し，または，甲に対し「特約店」に代わって

該従業員に対しこれを強制することを認める。

　e．本第7項による「特約店」の義務の違反は金銭による損害賠償によって適切に補償されるものではなく，甲は本第7項による「特約店」の義務の履行を特に強制するため差止命令その他適正な裁判所の命令を請求する権利を有するものとする。

　f．本第7条項による「特約店」の義務は本契約終了後も存続する。

【例　文】

8. Term and Termination:

　ａ．This agreement will terminate on ＿＿＿＿＿＿ unless earlier terminated.

　ｂ．"KO" or Distributor may terminate this agreement at any time upon not less than 90 days' prior notice.

　ｃ．This agreement will terminate immediately without notice by either party, (1) if Distributor becomes insolvent, (2) if an application is filed against Distributor for bankruptcy or for commencement of reorganization under the Commercial Code or the Corporate Reorganization Law or special liquidation, or if Distributor files an application for bankruptcy or for commencement of reorganization under the Commercial Code or the Corporate Reorganization Law, special liquidation or composition, or (3) if Distributor becomes subject "disposition for suspension of transaction" by a clearing house.

　ｄ．No indemnities or other compensation will be paid or payable to Distributor as a result of termination of this agreement and Distributor hereby waives any rights thereto which Distributor may have or hereafter acquire under any applicable laws. Any such termination, however, shall not affect any sums owing by Distributor to "KO" or by "KO" to Distributor as of the date of termination.

【語句の説明】

terminate：自動詞なら終了する，他動詞なら……を解除する
earlier termination：より早い終了；すなわち終了前の途中の解除
without notice：催告なしに

第3章　特約店・代理店契約

either party：いずれか一方の当事者
become insolvent：支払い不能状態になる
an application is filed against Distributor：特約店が……の申し立てを受ける
commencement of reorganization：更正手続きの開始
Corporate Reorganization Law：会社更正法
special liquidation：特別の整理
Distributor files an application：特約店が……の申し立てをする
disposition for suspension of transaction：取引停止処分
clearing house：手形交換所
compensation：補償
waive：放棄する
hereafter：今後，将来；hereinafter「以下」と混合しないこと
any sum owing by…to…：……が……に対して負う債務額
as of the date of the termination：終了の日現在

【訳　文】

8．有効期間および契約の終了：

　a．本契約は，先に解除された場合を別として＿＿＿＿＿＿に終了する。

　b．甲または特約店は90日以上前に予告して，いつでも本契約を終了せしめることができる。

　c．本契約は次の場合には，いずれか一方の当事者は本契約を催告なしに直ちに終了せしめるものとする。

　　(1)「特約店」が支払不能状態に至ったとき。

　　(2)「特約店」が破産，商法または会社更正法に基づく更正手続きの開始，あるいは特別整理を申し立てられ，または破産，商法または会社更正法に基づく更正手続きの開始，特別整理，和議の申し立てをしたとき。

　　(3)「特約店」が手形交換所より取引停止処分を受けたとき。

　d．本契約の終了による損害賠償その他の補償は，「特約店」に対して支払われず，支払義務も発生せず，「特約店」は法律の適用により有しているが，または将来取得することのできる権利を放棄する。ただし，本契約の終了により，終了日における「特約店」の甲に対する債務額または甲の「特約店」に対する債務額には影響されない。

【例　文】

9. **Assignment**：This agreement may not be assigned by Distributor. A change in control of Distributor will be deemed an assignment.
10. **Notices**：All notices, acceptances and other communications will be in writing and will be deemed given when delivered or mailed.
11. **Amendment**：This agreement constitutes the entire agreement of the parties, supersedes all prior agreements and may be amended only in writing.
12. **Governing Law**：This agreement will be governed by the law of Japan.

【語句の説明】

change in control of……：……に対する支配の変更；in は日本訳では「の」とするとしっくりする。increase in～，decrease in～なども同様。

be deemed：みなす；この代わりに regard, treat を使う方が誤解されにくい。

governing law：準拠法；この直訳は applicable law であるが，governing law の方が自然な用法である。

【訳　文】

9. 譲　渡：「特約店」は，本契約の譲渡をすることはできない。「特約店」に対する支配の変更は譲渡とみなす。
10. 通　知：すべての通知，承諾その他の意思表示は文書をもって行い，配達または郵送されたときにそれがなされたとみなす。
11. 変　更：本契約書は当事者間の合意の全体をなし，両当事者間の一切の先の含意に代わるものとし，本契約は文書をもってのみ変更することができる。
12. 準拠法：本契約には日本国法が適用される。

【例　文】

13. Signature：

　　a．For:　　　　　　　　　　b．For Distributor:
　　　（Name）　　　　　　　　　　（Name）

　　　_____　　　_____

第3章　特約店・代理店契約

```
        (Title)                    (Title)
    _____           _____
        (Date)                     (Date)
    _____           _____
```

─【訳　文】──────────────────────
13．署　名：
　　a．甲：
　　　（氏名または名称）
　　　_____
　　　（肩書）
　　　_____
　　　（日付）
　　　_____

　　b．特約店：
　　　（氏名または名称）
　　　_____
　　　（肩書）
　　　_____
　　　（日付）
　　　_____

第2節　代理店契約

前節の特約店契約と共通の内容の部分が多く，語句も重複しているので，代理店契約に特有の部分だけを重点的に説明する。

【例　文】

AGENT AGREEMENT

1. **Parties**：
   a．Kabushiki Kaisha（"KO"）：
      Country or state in which organized：Japan
      Address：＿＿＿＿＿＿ Minato-ku, Tokyo
   b．Full corporate name or other name of agent（"Agent"）：
      ＿＿＿＿＿＿＿＿＿＿＿＿＿＿＿＿＿＿＿＿
      Country or state in which organized：＿＿＿＿＿＿＿
      Address：＿＿＿＿＿＿＿＿＿＿＿＿＿＿＿＿
      ＿＿＿＿＿＿＿＿＿＿＿＿＿＿＿＿＿＿＿＿

【訳　文】

代理店契約

1．当事者：
   a．甲株式会社（「甲」）：
      設立準拠法所属国または州：日本
      住所：東京都港区＿＿＿＿＿＿＿＿＿＿
   b．代理店の正式名称またはその他の名称（「代理店」）：＿＿＿＿＿
      設立準拠法所属国または州：＿＿＿＿＿＿＿＿＿＿
      住所：＿＿＿＿＿＿＿＿＿＿＿＿＿＿＿＿＿

第3章 特約店・代理店契約

【例　文】

2. **Effective Date of this Agreement**：_____
3. **KO Policy**：The policy of "KO" is to select respected and competent agents who have the ability to sell "KO" products in areas where "KO" determines that sales through agents are desirable. "KO" supports its agents by providing such marketing and technical advice, information, literature and other sales assistance as "KO" considers appropriate.
4. **Appointment of Agent: Non-exclusivity of Appointment**：
   a．"KO" hereby appoints the Agent as an agent of those "KO" products listed in Exhibit A (the "KO Products") for the territory described in Exhibit B (the "Territory"). The Agent hereby accepts such appointment.
   b．The appointment of the Agent will not preclude "KO" from appointing other agents for the "KO Products" within the Territory nor will "KO" be prevented from making direct sales of any "KO Products" to customers in the Territory.

【訳　文】

2．本契約発効日：_____
3．甲の方針：甲の方針は，甲が販売代理店を通しての販売が望ましいと認めた地域において甲の製品を販売する能力を有し，尊敬されかつ有能な特約代理店を選択することにある。甲は，甲が適切と考えるマーケッティング上もしくは技術上の助言，情報，文献，その他の販売に関する助力を提供することによって当該代理店を援助する。
4．代理店の指定・非独占的指定：
　　a．甲は，「代理店」を別表Bに記載した地域（「地域」）における，別表Aに記載した製品（「甲製品」）の代理店に指定する。「代理店」は該指定を承諾する。
　　b．代理店の指定は，甲が「該地域」における「甲製品」向けに，他の代理店を指定することを妨げるものではなく，また甲が「該地域」において顧客に対し製品の直接販売をすることを妨げるものではない。

第2節　代理店契約

【例　文】

5. Duties of Agent：

   a．Agent will actively promote the "KO Products" in the Territory. Agent will quote only such prices and other terms and conditions as are specified by "KO".

   b．Agent will transmit or request customers to transmit an orders to "KO" in such form as "KO" may prescribe. Each order will be subject to acceptance by "KO" and may be rejected for any reason.

   c．Agent will provide "KO" with such sales reports and other sales-related information as "KO" may request.

   d．Agent has no authority to act on behalf of "KO".

6. Commissions：

   a．"KO" will pay Agent a commission on all sales within the Territory which result from orders procured by Agent and accepted by "KO".

   b．The amount of the commission will be _____% of the net sales price (exclusive of freight, taxes and other charges) unless otherwise specified in Exhibit "KO".

   c．Commissions will be paid within 45 days after the end of each quarter based on sales occurring within the quarter, provided, however, no commission shall be payable until "KO" shall have received payment from the customer to whom the sales were made.

【語句の説明】

duties of agent：代理店の義務
will quote：引用する，通知する
specified by ……：……が明示した
transmit：提出する
request customers to transmit：顧客に提出するよう要求する
in such form as …… may prescribe：……が定める形式で
a commission on all sales：すべての販売に対する手数料
orders procured by Agent and accepted by ……：代理店が獲得し，……が承諾し

第3章 特約店・代理店契約

た注文
net sales price：純売上金額
exclusive of……：……を除く
freight：運賃
within……**days after the end of each quarter**：各四半期末から……日以内
shall be payable：支払うものとする
the customer to whom the sales were made：販売がなされた顧客

【訳　文】

5．代理店の義務

　a．［代理店］は積極的に「地域」において甲の製品を宣伝し販売するものとする*。

　b．［代理店］は甲の定める形式で，すべての注文を甲に提出，あるいは顧客に提出するよう要求するものとする。各注文は甲の承諾のいかんを条件とし，なんらかの理由により拒絶されることがある。

　c．［代理店］は，甲の請求ある場合には甲に対して販売報告書およびその他販売に関する情報を提出する。

　d．［代理店］は甲に代わって行為をする権限を有しない。

6．手数料

　a．甲は［地域］内において，［代理店］が獲得し甲が承諾した注文に起因するすべての販売に対して［代理店］に手数料を支払う。

　b．手数料の額は，別表Ａで別段の定めをした場合は別として，純売上金額（運賃，税金その他を除き）の＿＿＿＿％とする。

　c．手数料は，各四半期末から45日以内にその四半期内に発生する販売を基礎として支払われるものとする。ただし，甲が販売のなされた顧客から支払いを受けるまで，手数料は支払われないものとする。

　＊［代理店］は甲が明示した価格および条件のみを引用する。

【例　文】

7. Confidentiality：

　a．From time to time "KO" may disclose to Agent confidential information relating to the "KO's Product" ("Confidential Information"). Confidential

第 2 節　代理店契約

　　Information shall not include (1) any information which was already in the possession of Agent, as evidenced by its written records, at the time of the disclosure by "KO", (2) any information which is lawfully received by Agent from a third party which is not under a secrecy obligation to "KO", and (3) any information which, at the time of disclosure to Agent or thereafter, becomes public knowledge otherwise than through a breach of Agent's obligations under this agreement. All disclosures of Confidential Information shall be made, or confirmed, in writing and shall be marked "Company Confidential" or with some label indicating their confidentiality.

ｂ．Agent agrees not to disclose any Confidential Information to any third party unless such disclosure shall be approved in writing by "KO".

ｃ．Agent shall not use any such Confidential Information except as may be necessary or appropriate to carry out its responsibilities under this agreement.

ｄ．Agent may disclose Confidential Information to those of its employees who have a need to know such information to carry out the duties of Agent under this agreement, provided that each such employee

　(1) shall be informed of Agent's responsibility under this agreement with respect to such information, and

　(2) shall have agreed in writing to hold confidential, and not disclose or use, any information obtained in the course of his or her employment.

　　Agent agrees, upon written request from "KO", to enforce against any such employee, or permit "KO" to enforce against any such employee on Agent's behalf, employee's obligations of confidentiality.

ｅ．Any violation by Agent of its obligations pursuant to this section 7 shall not be adequately compensable by monetary damages and "KO" shall be entitled to an injunction or other appropriate decree specifically enforcing Agent's obligations pursuant to this section 7.

ｆ．Agent's obligations under this section 7 shall survive any termination of this agreement.

第3章　特約店・代理店契約

【語句の説明】

agree not to disclose……：開示しないことに合意する

unless such disclosure shall be approved：そのような開示が許される場合は別として

in writing：書面により

except as may be necessary：必要な場合，必要である場合

have a need to know……：知る必要がある

upon written request from……：……の書面による要求により

obligation of confidentiality：秘密保持義務

monetary damages：金銭による損害賠償；damagesと複数になっているので損害賠償金を指す。単数なら，単に損害賠償。

be entitled to……：……の権利を有する

decree specifically enforcing……：特に……を強制する裁判所の命令

survive：本来の意味は，生き残る，それから転じて……の後も存続する

【訳　文】

7．秘密保持：

a．甲は「代理店」に対し，随時「甲」製品に関する機密である秘密情報（「秘密情報」）を開示する。「秘密情報」は以下の情報を含まないものとする。

(1) 甲によって開示された時に，すでに「代理店」が占有していたことが文書による記録によって証明できる情報

(2) 甲に対して秘密保持の義務を有しない第三者から「代理店」が適法に受領した情報

(3) 「代理店」に対して開示されたとき，またはそれ以降に本契約による「代理店」の義務の不履行によることなく公知となった情報

　　機密情報の開示はすべて書面によってなされ，または書面により確認され，かつ "Company Confidential" と表示されるかまたは秘密である旨のラベルで表示される。

b．「代理店」は，甲によって書面により許された場合は別として，第三者に対し秘密情報の開示をしないことに合意する。

c．「代理店」は本契約に基づく責任の履行に必要または適切である場合を

除き，「秘密情報」を使用しない。
  d．「代理店」は，従業員が本契約に基づく「代理店」の義務を履行するために秘密情報を知る必要がある従業員に対し，「秘密情報」を開示することができる。ただし，以下の場合に限る。
    (1) 当該各従業員に対し，当該情報に関して本契約に基づく「代理店」の義務を知らしてある場合
    (2) 当該各従業員が職務に関し取得した情報を秘密とし，開示しないこと，および使用しないことを文書によって合意している場合
    「代理店」は，甲から文書により要求があった場合，該従業員に対して従業員の秘密保持義務を強制し，または甲に対し，「代理店」に代わって該従業員に対しこれを強制することを認める。
  e．本第5項による「代理店」の義務の違反は金銭による損害賠償によって補償し得るものではなく，甲は，本第5項による「代理店」の義務の履行を特に強制するため差止め命令またはその他適切な裁判所の命令を請求する権利を有するものとする。
  f．本第5条項による代理店の義務は本契約終了後も存続する。

【例　文】

8. **Term and Termination**：
   a．This agreement will terminate on _____ unless earlier terminated.
   b．"KO" or Agent may terminate this agreement at any time upon not less than 90 days'prior notice.
   c．This agreement will terminate immediately without notice by either party, (1) if Agent becomes insolvent, (2) if an application is filed against Agent for bankruptcy or for commencement of reorganization under the Commercial Code or the Corporate Reorganization Law or special liquidation, or if Agent files an application for bankruptcy or for commencement of reorganization under the Commercial Code or the Corporate Reorganization Law, special liquidation or composition, or (3) if Agent becomes subject to "disposition for suspension of transaction" by a clearing house.
   d．No indemnities or other compensation will be paid or payable to Agent as

第3章　特約店・代理店契約

a result of termination of this agreement and Agent hereby waives any rights thereto which Agent may have or hereafter acquire under any applicable laws. Any such termination, however, shall not affect any sums owing by Agent to "KO" or by "KO" to Agent as of the date of termination.

9. **Assignment**： This agreement may not be assigned by Agent. A change in control of Agent will be deemed an assignment.

―【訳　文】―
8．有効期間および契約の終了：
　　a．本契約は先に解除された場合は別として，＿＿＿＿＿に終了する。
　　b．甲または代理店は90日以上前に予告していつでも本契約を終了せしめることができる。
　　c．本契約は次の場合には，いずれか一方の当事者は本契約を催告なしに，直ちに終了せしめるものとする。
　　　(1)「代理店」が支払い不能状態に至ったとき。
　　　(2)「代理店」が破産，商法または会社更正法に基づく更正手続きの開始，あるいは特別整理を申し立てられ，または破産，商法または会社更正法に基づく更正手続きの開始，特別整理，和議の申し立てをしたとき。
　　　(3)「代理店」が手形交換所より取引停止処分をうけたとき。
　　d．本契約の終了による損害賠償その他の補償は，「代理店」に対して支払われず，支払い義務も発生せず，「代理店」は法律の適用により有し，または株主取得することできる一切の権利をここに放棄する。ただし本契約の終了により，終了日における「代理店」の甲に対する債務額または甲の「代理店」に対する債務額には影響されない。
9．譲　渡：「代理店」は本契約の譲渡をすることはできない。「代理店」に対する支配の変更は譲渡とみなす。

―【例　文】―
10. **Notices**： All notices, acceptances and other communications will be in writing and will be deemed given when delivered or mailed.
11. **Amendment**： This agreement constitutes the entire agreement of the

parties, supersedes all prior agreements and may be amended only in writing.
12. **Governing Law**：This agreement will be governed by the law of Japan.
13. **Signature**：

 a．For:
  (Name)
  _____

  (Title)
  _____

  (Date)
  _____

 b．For Agent:
  (Name)
  _____

  (Title)
  _____

  (Date)
  _____

【訳　文】

10．通　知：すべての通知，承諾その他の意思表示は文書をもって行い，配達または輸送されたとさにそれがなされたとみなす。

11．変　更：本契約書は当事者間の合意の全体をなし，両当事者間の一切の先の合意に替わるものとし，本契約は文書をもってのみ変更することができる。

12．準拠法：本契約には日本は法が適用される。

13．署　名：

 a．甲：
  (氏名または名称)
  _____

  (肩書)
  _____

  (日付)
  _____

 b．代理店：
  (氏名または名称)
  _____

  (肩書)
  _____

  (日付)
  _____

第3節　売買契約

ここでは，日本での売買契約書を例に，いくつかに分解して英訳してみる。

【例　文】

売買基本契約書

甲株式会社(以下，甲という)と乙株式会社(以下，乙という)とは，将来継続して甲の販売する商品(以下，単に物品という)を売買するために，次の通り基本契約を締結した。

第1条　この契約に定める事項のうち，個別的売買に関するもの(第4条ないし第16条)はこの契約の有効期間中，甲乙間に締結される一切の売買契約につき，その内容として共通に適用されるものとする。ただし，個別的契約においてこの契約に定める事項の一部もしくは全部の適用を排除し，またはこの契約と異なる事項を有することを妨げない。

【語句の説明】

基本売買契約書：MASTER SALES CONTRACT. 基本労務契約ならMASTER LABOR CONTRACT. また，その意味をとってGENERAL TERMS AND CONDITIONS FOR SALES OF GOODSとも訳せる。

以下……という：hereinafter referred to as……; hereinafterとhereafterを混同しないこと。hereinafterは「以下」, hereafterは「将来」。

株式会社：通常はCo., Ltd.としている。ここではCo., Ltd.としたが，厳密に考えると，その意味をとりjoint-stock companyとすべきであるとし，また，日本の株式会社を正確に表現する英語がないから，Kabushiki KaishaあるいはK.K.とすべきであるという人もいる。

　有限会社(limited company)は，イギリスのprivate companyと非常に似ているの。なお，private companyとprivate corporationとは異なることに留意されたい。前者はイギリスの会社法上の会社であるのに対し，後者はpublic corporation(公法人)に対するもので，純粋の公の目的と区別された非営利目的で設立された私

法人である。ただし，後者の意味でbusiness corporationと同様に用いられることが多い。

【語句の説明】

甲株式会社：KO Kabushiki Kaisha；いずれにしても会社名は翻訳者が勝手に訳きずに，当事者である会社の正式な英文名を使用すること。

将来継続して：continuously……for the future

以下単に……という：hereinafter simply referred to as……

この契約に定める事項：any provision of this agreement

個別契約に関する：relating to separate sales, relating to individual sales

第4条ないし第16条：Article 4 to Article 16, inclusive；あるいはArticles 4 to 16, inclusive. inclusiveは，4条および16条を含ませる意味で使われる。

この契約の有効期間中：during the effective period of this agreement

一切の売買契約：any and all sales agreements；anyかall, いずれか単独でもかまわないようであるが，契約書では通常これらを一組にしてany and allとする。

……として共通に適用される：commonly apply to……

ただし：however, providing that……

一部もしくは全部：in whole or in part

……の適用を排除し：preclude the application of……

……異なる：contrary to……

有する：「包含させる」と言い換えてcontainを使う。

次に示す〔訳文A〕は日本語の原文に忠実なことを主眼として，作成されたものである。〔訳文B〕は，その点を多少緩やかに考えて作成されたもので，実際に使われているものである。以下の訳例でも同様である。

【訳文A】

MASTER SALES CONTRACT

THIS AGREEMENT is made this ___ day of ___ , 1991, by and between KO Kabushiki Kaisha having its principal place of business at Tokyo, Japan, (hereinafter referred to as "KO") and OTSU Kabushiki Kaisha having its principal place of business at ___ (hereinafter referred to as "OTSU")

pertaining to certain goods which KO would continuously sell to OTSU for the future (hereinafter simply referred to as "goods").

Article 1. Any provision of this agreement relating to separate sales (Article 4 to Article 16, inclusive) shall commonly apply to any and all sales agreements (pertaining to separate sales) concluded between KO and OTSU during the effective period of this agreement, providing this shall not prevent the separate agreement from precluding the application in whole or in part of the provisions hereof, or from containing any matters therein contrary to this agreement.

【訳文B】

GENERAL TERMS AND CONDITIONS FOR SALES OF GOODS

KO Kabushiki Kaisha having its principal place of business at Tokyo, Japan, (hereinafter referred to as "KO") and OTSU Kabushiki Kaisha having its principal place of business at ＿＿ (hereinafter referred to as "OTSU") agree to the terms and conditions of the sales of certain goods which KO will sell to OTSU in the future under Article 2 hereof (hereinafter simply referred to as "goods").

Article 1. Provisions in this agreement relating to individual sales (Article 4 to Article 15, inclusive) shall commonly apply to any and all individual sales made by KO to OTSU during the effective period of this agreement, unless different arrangement is made for a particular sale.

【解　説】
〔訳文B〕では，後半の部分を「特定の売買について，異なった取り決めをした場合は別として」と考えて，「unless different arrangement is made for a particular sale」とした。unless は，契約書では unless＝if not と考えて，「もし……でないならば」などとしないで「……の場合は別として」とすると分かりやすい。

また，**Article 4 to Article 15, inclusive** としてあるのは，実際に用いる契約書では

第6条を削除し，条項が1条ずつ繰り上がっているからである。

[注] 契約書の日付は，日本文では末尾にくるが，英文では最初にもってきて末尾の部分で「as of the day and year first above written」と書かれていることが多い。

【例　文】

第2条　この契約に基づく売買の目的となる物品は＿＿＿＿＿＿とする。

第3条　甲から乙に対して売渡される物品の品名，数量，単価，引き渡し条件，代金支払期限，方法，その他売買に必要な条件はこの契約に定めるものを除き，個別売買の都度，甲乙間において別に締結される売買契約によって定める。

　2　前項の売買契約は，乙の提出する注文書と甲の交付する注文請書の交換によって成立する。この場合には，甲の注文請書の交付の時に個別的売買契約が成立する。

【語句の説明】

この契約に基づく：under this agreement

売買の目的となる：「売買の目的(物)を構成する」と考えてconstituting the subject-matter of salesとする。目的はobjectとせず，subject-matterとする。subject-matterが必ずしも「主題」，「主体」だけを指すと考えないことである。

　英語では，日本語の「目的」と「主題」がいつも「subject」と「object」にならないことに注意。たとえば，the subject-matter of inventionは「発明の主題」でなく「発明の対象」と解釈する。また，民法第304条第1項の中で「其目的物の売却……により，債務者が受くべき金銭」を「……the money……which the obligors entitled to receive……by reason of the sale……of……the subject-matter」と英訳されている。

品名：specification of goods, description of goods

数量：quantity

単価：unit price

引き渡し条件：delivery conditions

代金支払期限，方法：date and method of payment

その他売買につき必要な条件：any other conditions necessary for sales, any other

第3章　特約店・代理店契約

terms and conditions of sale
この契約に定めるもの：those provided for hereunder
前項の：in the preceding paragraph
成立する：take effect
……と……を交換する：exchange……with……
注文書：a written order
注文請書：a written acceptance of order
交付する：deliver, serve；送付（名詞）なら service

【訳文A】

Article 2. The goods constituting the subject matter of sales under this agreement shall be _____ .

Article 3. The specification of goods, quantity, unit price, delivery conditions, date and method of payment, and any other conditions necessary for sales concerning the goods to be sold by KO to OTSU shall be, except those provided for hereunder, determined in the sale agreement for each separate sale concluded between KO and OTSU.

 2 The sales agreement in the preceding paragraph shall take effect by exchanging a written order submitted by OTSU with a written acceptance of order given by KO. In this instance, the separate sales agreement takes effect when KO serves the written acceptance of order on OTSU.

【訳文B】

Article 2. The goods whose sales are to be covered by this agreement are: _____ .

Article 3. The description of goods, quantity, unit price, delivery conditions, date and method of payment, and any other terms and conditions of individual sale from KO to OTSU that are not provided in this agreement shall be determined by the parties on the occasion of each individual sale.

 2 The individual sale shall take effect upon delivery by KO to OTSU of written acceptance of the order placed by OTSU.

【解 説】
〔訳文B〕では同じ内容のこと（第3条第2項）を一つのセンテンスで表現している。

【例　文】

第4条　物品の引き渡し前に生じた物品の滅失，毀損，減量，変質，その他一切の損害は，乙の責に帰すべきものを除き甲の負担とし，物品の引き渡し後に生じたこれらの損害は，甲の責に帰すべきものを除き乙の負担とする。

第5条　甲は，個別的契約に定める約定期限に約定引き渡し場所に物品を持参し乙に引き渡し，乙は物品受け取り後10日以内に物品を検査する。

　　2　物品の受け渡しは，乙の検査終了と同時に完了する。検査の遅延により甲に生じた損害は乙の負担とする。

　　3　物品の所有権は，物品の受け渡しがあったときに甲から乙に移転する。ただし，特約ある場合には代金の弁済が完了する時まで物品の所有権は移転しない。

【語句の説明】

物品の引き渡し前：prior to the delivery of goods

滅失：loss

毀損：destruction

減量：reduction in quantity；「in」の使い方に注意。日本語の「の」が英語では「in」になる例が多くある。たとえば「量の増加」increase in quantity，「量の変化」change in quantity，「量の減少」decrease in quantity, reduction in quantity

変質：deterioration

その他の損害：any other damage；damagesと複数形にすると損害賠償金のこと。

……の責めに帰する：imputable to……

……の負担とする：be liable for……

これらの損害：単にsuch damageとしないで，物品の引き渡し前に生じた滅失等と後でのそれとのバランスをとるために，such damage of similar natureとする。

個別契約で定める：fixed by the separate sales agreement.〔訳文B〕では，個別契約のために合意したという主旨で英訳した。

第3章　特約店・代理店契約

持参し……引き渡し：transport and deliver

物品を検査する：inspect the goods

受け取り後：as from the day of receipt thereof. thereofはof itと同じ。原文では「受取日」とはなっていないが，「10日以内」となっているので，「受け取った日からの」の意に解し，訳文では「day」を補ってある。

物品の受け渡しは……完了する：the delivery of goods shall be completed.

検査の遅延：delay in the inspection この場合の「の」も「of」ではなく「in」である。

甲に生じた損害：damage inflicted upon KO

……から……に移転する：pass from……to……

特約ある場合：in the presence of special agreement, if so specifically agreed upon ; 特約のない場合：in the absence of special agreement

---【訳文A】---

Article 4. KO shall be liable for any damage arising out of the loss, destruction, reduction in quantity and deterioration, or any other damage to goods prior to the delivery of goods, except those imputable to OTSU, and OTSU shall be liable for such damage of similar nature caused subsequent to the delivery of goods except that imputable to KO.

Article 5. KO shall transport and deliver the goods to OTSU at the place fixed by the separate sales agreement, and OTSU shall inspect the goods within 10 days as from the date of receipt thereof.

　2　The delivery of goods shall be completed when OTSU completes the inspection thereof. OTSU shall be liable for damage inflicted upon KO because of any delay in the inspection.

　3　The title to goods shall pass from KO to OTSU when the delivery of goods is completed. However, the title to goods shall remain, if in the presence of special agreement, with KO until the full payment is made.

---【訳文B】---

Article 4. KO shall be liable for loss, destruction, reduction in quantity, deterioration of goods, or any other damage to the goods which took place prior to the delivery thereof, except for such imputable to OTSU, and

第3節 売買契約

> OTSU shall be liable for damage of similar nature caused subsequent to the delivery of goods except for such imputable to KO.
>
> **Article 5.** KO shall deliver the goods to OTSU at the place and the time agreed upon for the (individual) sale thereof. OTSU shall inspect the goods within 10 days from the date of receipt thereof.
>
> 2 The delivered goods shall be considered to have been accepted at the time when OTSU completes inspection thereof. OTSU shall be liable for damage inflicted upon KO because of any delay in the inspection.
>
> 3 The title to goods shall pass from KO to OTSU at the time that the delivered goods are accepted by OTSU. However, the title to goods shall remain with KO until the full payment is made if so specifically agreed upon by the parties for the sale.

【例 文】

第6条 甲は，不合格品または契約数量を超過した部分および契約を解除された物品その他，乙より返却できる物品を自分の費用をもって乙の通知発送の日から10日以内に引き取らなければならない。

 2 前項の期間経過後において甲の引き取りがない場合に，乙は甲の費用をもって物品を返却もしくは供託し，または物品を売却してその代価を保管もしくは供託できる。

第7条 売買代金は，個別契約にしたがい支払期限に現金，小切手または約束手形で支払う。

 2 約束手形または小切手により支払いがなされた場合において，その手形または小切手の決済が完了するまでは債務弁済の効力は生じない。

 3 手形による支払いが認められた場合においても，第11条の各号の1に該当する事実が発生したときは，甲の請求により乙はいつでも現金にて弁済する。

【語句の説明】

不合格品：rejected goods, off-grade goods, goods rejected
契約数量：the quantity agreed upon

第3章　特約店・代理店契約

……を超過した部分：any portion……, in excess of……
契約を解除された物品：goods cancelled
返却できる物品：goods to be returned
自分の費用で：at my own expense, at its own expense
通知発送：the dispatch of a notice
引取る：take back
期間経過後：after the expiration of the period of time
甲の引き取りがない場合：if KO does not take back……
返却し：return, send back
代価を保管し：この場合の代価はpriceやmoneyにせず，keep the proceedsとする。
供託する：deposit……with the competent authorities
売買代金：purchase money, purchase price；英語では売買のことをsale and purchaseと言わず，単にsaleとする。同様に，売買代金の場合sale and purchase moneyとせず，purchase moneyとする。
……で(により)支払う：pay in……
約束手形：promissory note；為替手形ならbill of exchange
個別契約にしたがい支払期限に：意味のとり方により訳し方が異なる。一つは個別契約で定めた日と解し，on a day as specified in the separate agreementとする。あるいは，個別契約の条件にしたがい支払日にと解し，on the day in accordance with the terms of the individual saleとする。termもconditionも条件を指すと解されているが，conditionは条件一般を指し，termは金銭に関する条件を指すと言われている。
場合において：if
……の決済が完了するまで：until the settlement of……is completed
手形による支払い：the payment in the promissory note, payment of promissory note
……の請求により：upon the request of……

【解　説】
〔訳文A〕については，この場合の最初の日本文のドラフトでは，日本の典型的な雛型を示すために第6条を書いたので，甲にとって不利な条項も入っている。そこで，本社の方で削除するように指示した。そのため〔訳文B〕ではその部分が存在しない。

第 3 節　売買契約

> 【訳文 A】
>
> **Article 6.**　KO shall, within 10 days from the dispatch of a notice from OTSU, take back, at its own expense, goods rejected or any portion of goods in excess of the quantity agreed upon, goods cancelled and any other goods to be returned.
>
> 　2　If KO does not take back the goods after the expiration of the period of time in the preceding paragraph, OTSU may, at the expense of KO, send back or deposit the goods with the competent authorities, or sell the goods and keep the proceeds thereof or deposit the same with the competent authorities.
>
> **Article 7.**　The purchase money shall be paid either in cash, check or promissory note on a day as specified in the separate agreement.
>
> 　2　If the payment is made in a promissory note or check, the performance of obligation shall not take effect until the settlement of the promissory note or check is completed.
>
> 　3　If there arises any fact coming under any item of Article 11, OTSU shall pay KO in cash at any time, upon the request of the latter, even if the payment in the promissory note is agreed.

> 【訳文 B】
>
> **Article 6.**　The purchase price shall be paid in cash, by check or by promissory note on the due date in accordance with the terms of the individual sale.
>
> 　2　If the payment is made by a promissory note or check, the goods shall not be considered as having been paid for until the settlement of the promissory note or check.
>
> 　3　If any fact arises which comes under any item of Article 10, OTSU shall pay KO in cash at any time, upon request of the latter, even if payment by promissory note has been agreed.

　ここでは、原文の第 6 条に削除されたので英訳文は存在せず、第 7 条が繰り上って第 6 条となっている。以下同じ。

第3章　特約店・代理店契約

【例　文】

第8条　甲が乙に対して債務を負担しているときは，甲は本件債権の弁済期の到来すると否とを問わず，本件債権と甲が乙に対して負担する債務の対等額につき相殺することができる。

第9条　甲は，乙に対して有する債権を第三者に譲渡することができる。

第10条　乙が売買代金債務の支払いを怠ったときは，乙は甲に対して支払期日の翌日より完済の日まで，日歩銭の割合による遅延損害金を支払う。

第11条　次の各号の場合に，甲は乙に対して直ちに債務の全部の支払いを請求できる。

【語句の説明】

債務を負担する：assume an obligation
債権弁済期の到来する：債務が弁済期にあると言い換えて，a claim is due
本件：hereunder
否と問わず：regardless of whether……or not
本件債権と……相殺する：set off the claim hereunder
甲が乙に対して負担する：KO's obligation to OTSU
対等額：corresponding amount
第三者：third party, third person
譲渡する：assign；「移転する」なら transfer
売買代金債務：purchase money
……の支払いを怠る：in negligence of the payment of……
支払期日の翌日から：from the day after the date of payment
完済の日まで：to the date of the complete payment thereof
日歩……銭：……Sen per day for ￥100；日歩とだけあり，原文に記載されていないが，「100円につき」を補って英訳すること。
……の割合による：at the rate of……
遅延損害金：penalty
次の各号の場合：「次の各号に該当する場合」と考えて，in any case coming under any item mentioned below, any of the following cases

118

第3節　売買契約

債務の全部：the whole obligation
請求できる：may demand
直ちに：immediately
一時に：「一括して」と考えて，in a lump sum

【訳文A】

Article 8.　When KO assumes an obligation to OTSU, KO may, regardless of whether or not any claim hereunder is due, set off the claim hereunder against KO's obligation to OTSU, so far as the corresponding amount is concerned.

Article 9.　KO may assign any claim against OTSU to any third party.

Article 10.　When OTSU is in negligence of the payment of the purchase money, OTSU shall pay KO a penalty at the rate of ＿＿ Sen per day for each ￥100 after the date on which payment is due until full payment is made.

Article 11.　In any case coming under any item below-mentioned, KO may demand OTSU to pay the whole obligation immediately.

【訳文B】

Article 7.　When KO has a debt to OTSU for any reason whatsoever, KO may offset such debt against its claim toward OTSU hereunder to the extent of the corresponding amount, regardless of whether or not such claim is due.

Article 8.　KO may assign any claim hereunder against OTSU to any third party.

Article 9.　Should OTSU fail to pay the purchase price, OTSU shall pay KO a penalty at the rate of —— Sen per day per ￥100 from the day immediately following the due date of payment to the day of completion of payment.

Article 10.　In any of the following cases, OTSU shall pay to KO immediately its whole obligation hereunder in a lump sum upon KO's demand:

【解　説】

　〔訳文B〕の場合は，第10条（原文の第11条が繰り上がって第10条になっている）の原文を若干修正のうえ英訳している。すなわち，「甲は乙に対して」を削除し，

第3章 特約店・代理店契約

「甲の請求をうけたとき乙は」とし、「債務の」の次に「金額を一時に弁済しなければならない」を挿入し、さらに「全部の支払いを請求できる」を削除している。

【例　文】
(1) 乙が甲に対する個別的契約上の売買代金支払い債務その他一切の債務につき支払い義務を怠ったとき。
(2) 乙が差し押さえ、仮差し押さえ、仮処分の申し立てを受け、あるいは公売処分、租税滞納処分その他の公権力の処分を受けまたは整理、会社更正手続きの開始、破産もしくは公売を申し立てられ、または自ら和議、会社更正手続きの開始もしくは破産の申し立てをしたとき。
(3) 乙が、監督官庁より営業停止または営業免許もしくは営業登録の取り消しの処分を受けたとき
(4) 乙が資本減少、営業の廃止もしくは変更、または解散、組織変更の協議をしたとき。
(5) 乙が手形交換所より銀行取引停止処分を受け、その他支払い停止状態に至ったとき。
(6) 乙が個別的契約の条項に違反したとき。
(7) その他、乙の財産状態が悪化し、またはその恐れがあると認められる相当の事由があるとき。

【語句の説明】

……を怠る：in negligence of

差し押さえ：attachment

仮差し押さえ：provisional attachment

仮処分：provisional disposition

……の申立：a motion for……；move は motion の動詞で「申し立てる」

申し立てを受ける：be subjected to a motion；現在ではむしろこのような使い方が多い。たとえば、最近受け取った米国の破産裁判所からの通知の中に次のような類似の語句の使い方があった。

　"……Attendance by creditors at the meeting is <u>welcomed</u>, but not required." その趣旨は、「債権者会議への出席は歓迎するが要求されない」ということである。見慣れている英語ではwelcomedではなくwelcomeであろう。

第 3 節　売買契約

公売処分：a disposition for public auction
租税滞納処分：disposition for default in tax payment
公権力の処分：a disposition by public authorities
整理：application for reorganization
会社更正手続きの開始：an institution of reorganization under the Corporation Reorganization Law
破産もしくは公売の申し立て：an application for bankruptcy or public auction
和議：composition
自ら……申立てをする：by itself applies
監督官庁：the competent supervising government office
営業停止：suspension of business
営業の取り消し：cancellation of business license
資本の減少：reduction in capital
営業の廃止：discontinuance of business
解散：dissolution
組織変更：change in organization
協議をする：take a procedure for……
手形交換所：a clearing house
銀行取引停止処分：the disposition for the suspension of banking transactions
支払い停止状態に至る：「支払い不能になる」と言い換えて，become insolvent
……条項に違反する：in contravention of any provision of……
財産状態が悪化する：financial status is aggravated
その恐れがあると認められる相当の事由：a good reason to believe such, a good reason to believe such is likely to occur

---

【訳文 A】

(1) when OTSU is in negligence of the payment of the purchase money as specified by the separate agreement and/or any other payment,

(2) when OTSU is subjected to a motion for attachment, provisional attachment and provisional disposition, or to a disposition for public auction, disposition for default in tax payment or any other dispositions by public authorities, or to an institution of reorganization under the Corporation Reorganization Law or

121

第3章 特約店・代理店契約

otherwise, or subjected to an application for bankruptcy or public auction, or by itself applies for an application for composition, the institution of corporate reorganization under the Corporation Reorganization Law,

(3) when OTSU is subjected to such disposition as for the suspension of business, or cancellation of its business license or business registration by the competent supervising government office,

(4) when OTSU takes a procedure for the reduction in capital, discontinuance or change of business, dissolution or change in organization,

(5) when OTSU is subjected to the disposition for the suspension of banking transactions by a clearing house,

(6) when OTSU is in contravention of any provision of the separate agreement,

(7) In addition, when OTSU's financial status is aggravated or there is a good reason to believe such.

【訳文B】

(1) if OTSU is negligent in its payment for the goods under any individual sales and/or performance of any other obligations toward KO,

(2) if OTSU becomes subject to attachment, provisional attachment or provisional disposition, or to a public auction by public authorities, to disposition due to default in tax payment or to any other disposition by public authorities or to application for composition or reorganization under the Commercial Code or the Corporate Reorganization Law, or to application for bankruptcy or public auction, or if OTSU itself applies for composition, bankruptcy or commencement of corporate reorganization under the Commercial Code or the Corporate Reorganization Law,

(3) if OTSU becomes subject to any disposition, such as, suspension of business, or cancellation of its business license or of its business registration by the competent supervising government agencies,

(4) if OTSU reduces its capital, discontinues or changes its business or dissolves or changes its organization,

(5) if OTSU becomes subject to "disposition for suspension of transaction" by a

clearing house, or becomes insolvent,
(6) if OTSU is in contravention of any of the terms of individual sales, or
(7) if OTSU's financial status has deteriorated or if there is a good reason to believe such is likely to occur.

【例　文】
第12条　乙が引き渡し期日に物品を引き取らない等，契約の履行を怠った場合は，甲はいつでもその物品を乙の計算において任意に処分の上，その売得金をもって乙に対する損害賠償権を含む一切の債権の弁済に充当し，不足額があるときは乙に請求できる。
　　2　前項の場合において，他の個別的契約による引き渡すべき物品があるときは，その引き渡し期限が到来していないものについても同様とする。
第13条　甲は，引き渡し前の原因によって生じた物品の品質不良，変質その他の瑕疵についても乙の検査に合格したもの，または異議を留めず乙が受領したものについては，その責に任じない。
　　2　物品に直ちに発見することのできない瑕疵を引き渡し日から6ケ月以内に発見し，かつその旨を書面により甲に直ちに通知した場合に限り，乙はその契約の解除または代品納入，瑕疵の補修もしくは代金減額および損害のある場合には損害賠償を請求できる。

【語句の説明】

物品を引取らない：failure to take delivery of goods
引き渡し期日：the delivery date
いつでも：at any time
乙の計算において：on account of OTSU
任意に：arbitrarily
任意に処分する：arbitrarily dispose of……
売得金：the proceeds
充当する：appropriate
不足額があるとき：when……is insufficient

第 3 章　特約店・代理店契約

引き渡すべき物品：goods to be delivered
引き渡し期限が到来していないもの：goods the delivery date of which is not due yet
同様とする：this shall likewise apply to ……
品質不良：deficiency in quality
変質：deterioration in quality
乙の検査に合格する：pass OTSU's inspection
異議を留めず：without raising an objection
乙が受領する：OTSU takes the delivery of ……
直ちに発見することのできない瑕疵：a defect which is not immediately discoverable
書面により：in writing
直ちに通知する：immediately advise
場合に限り：only if
契約の解除：the cancellation of agreement
代品の納入：the delivery of substitute goods
瑕疵の補修：curing of defects，病気の治療も法律用語の治癒も cure
代金の減額：reduction in price
損害賠償を請求する：claim damages

【訳文Ａ】

Article 12.　When OTSU is in negligence of the performance of the obligation provided for in any agreements such as, for example, failure to take the delivery of goods on the delivery date, KO may arbitrarily dispose of the goods at any time on account of OTSU and then appropriate the proceeds thereof to KO's claims against OTSU, including any claims for damage and may demand further payment when such is insufficient.

2　In the case of the preceding paragraph, when there are any other goods to be delivered under a separate agreement, this shall likewise apply to those goods, the delivery date of which is not due yet.

Article 13.　KO shall not be liable for any defects in the goods such as any deficiency or deterioration in quality caused prior to the date of delivery, if such goods have passed OTSU's inspection or if OTSU took the delivery thereof without raising an objection.

第3節　売買契約

2　If OTSU discovers a defect which was not immediately discoverable in the goods within six months from the date of delivery thereof and only if OTSU immediately advises KO of this fact in writing, may OTSU demand the cancellation of the agreement, the delivery of substitute goods, curing of the defects or reduction in price, and claim damages if occasioned.

【訳文B】

Article 11.　If OTSU fails to accept delivery of goods on the delivery date or otherwise fails to perform any of its obligations hereunder or under any individual sales, KO may arbitrarily dispose of the said goods at any time on the account of OTSU and then appropriate the proceeds thereof to KO's claims against OTSU, including claims for damages and may demand further payment of any deficiency.

2　Should the preceding paragraph apply and if there are any other goods to be delivered under an individual sale, this shall likewise apply to those goods even though the delivery date has not yet passed.

Article 12.　KO shall not be liable for any defects in the goods, such as, inferior quality or deterioration in quality caused by reasons existing prior to the delivery, if such goods have passed OTSU's inspection or if OTSU has accepted delivery thereof without raising any objections.

【解　説】

〔訳文B〕では，第12条（原契約書の第13条に相当）の第2項は，甲の都合から削除されているので，英訳されていない。

【例　文】

第14条　天変地異，戦争，暴動，内乱，法令の改廃制定，公権力による命令処分，同盟罷業その他の争議行為，輸送機関の事故その他不可抗力により契約の全部もしくは一部の履行の遅延，または引き渡しの不能の生じた場合，甲はその責に任じない。

2　この場合，その契約は引き渡し不能になった部分については消滅する。

125

第3章　特約店・代理店契約

> 第15条　第11条各号の1に該当する事実が発生したとき，甲は催告および自己の債務の履行の提供をしないで直ちに個別的契約を解除できる。なお，甲の損害賠償の請求を妨げない。
> 　2　甲が個別的契約の条項に違反し，または当該個別的契約および他の個別的契約上の債務の履行を怠ったとき，乙は催告および自己の債務の履行の提供をしないで，直ちに個別的契約を解除し，甲に対して損害賠償を請求できる。

【語句の説明】

天変地異：natural disaster
暴動：riot
内乱：internal disturbance, civil war
法令：laws and ordinances
法令の改廃：abolition and institution of laws and ordinances
公権力による命令処分：orders and dispositions by the exercise of government power, 「行使」の意味を補い exercise を加えた。
その他の争議行為：other labor disturbances
輸送機関の事故：transportation accidents
その他不可抗力：other acts of God, force majeure
履行の遅延：a delay to perform
……不能の生じた場合：when there is caused an in ability to perform
第11条各号の：any items of Article 11
事実が発生したとき：when there arises any fact, when any fact occurs
催告：peremptory notice, advance notice
債務履行の提供：offering the performance of its own obligation
……の請求を妨げない：this shall not prevent …… from ……

【訳文A】

Article 14.　When there is caused a delay or inability to perform in whole or in part the obligation of the agreement due to natural disaster, war, riot, internal disturbance, amendment, abolition or institution of laws and ordinances, orders and dispositions by the exercise of government power,

第 3 節　売買契約

strikes or other labor disturbances, transportation accidents or any other acts of God, KO shall not be liable for such delay or inability.

2　In such instance, this agreement shall cease to exist with respect to the portion which has become impossible to perform.

Article 15.　When there arises any fact coming under any items of Article 11, KO may terminate the separate agreement immediately without peremptory notice and without offering the performance of its own obligation. Further, this shall not prevent KO from claiming damages.

2　When KO is in contravention of any provisions of the separate agreement or is in negligence of the performance of its obligation under the said separate agreement and any other separate agreements, OTSU may terminate the separate agreement immediately, without a peremptory notice and without offering the performance of its obligation, and may claim damages against KO.

──【訳文 B】──────────────

Article 13.　KO shall not be liable for a delay or failure in delivery, in whole or in part, due to natural disasters, war, riots, civil war, amendment, abolition or enactment of laws or regulations, orders by government agencies, strikes or other labor disturbances, transportation accidents or any other acts of God.

2　In such an instance, the individual sales hall cease to exist with respect to that portion of the delivery that has become impossible.

Article 14.　When any fact coming under any item of Article 10 shall occur, KO may cancel any or all individual sales immediately without advance notice and without offering the performance of its own obligation. This shall not prevent KO from claiming damages.

【解　説】

〔訳文 B〕は，第 15 条（訳文 B では，第 14 条に該当）第 2 項は，さきに説明したのと同じ理由で削除されているので，その部分の英訳例は存在しない。

第3章　特約店・代理店契約

【例　文】

第16条　個別的契約により生ずる権利義務に関する訴訟については，東京地方裁判所をもって管轄裁判所とする。

第17条　この契約の有効期間は平成＿＿年＿＿月＿＿日より満＿＿年とする。

　　2　前項の期間満了＿＿月前までに当事者の一方または双方より，書面による変更または解約の申し入れのない場合には，この契約はさらに満＿＿年間自動的に更新されるものとし，以後も同様とする。

【語句の説明】

権利義務：rights and obligations

東京地方裁判所：the Tokyo District Court

管轄裁判所：the court having the jurisdiction over any litigation

期間満了前：before the expiration of the effective period

当事者の一方または双方：either or both parties

変更または解約の申入れ：request for an amendment or termination

自動的に更新される：shall be extended；敢えて自動的をautomaticallyと訳さなくても意味が通じるので省略する。

以後も同様とする：hereafter the same

【訳文A】

Article 16. The Tokyo District Court shall be the court having the jurisdiction over any litigation arising out of rights and obligations under the separate agreement.

Article 17. The effective period of this agreement is ＿＿ year(s) from ＿＿ to ＿＿ .

　　2　Unless either or both parties make request for an amendment or termination in writing ＿＿ months before the expiration of the effective period in the preceding paragraph, this agreement shall be further extended for the period of ＿＿ and hereafter the same.

【訳文B】

Article 15. The Tokyo District Courts hall be the court having jurisdiction over

第3節 売買契約

any litigation concerning rights and obligations under this individual sales hereunder.

Article 16. The effective period of this agreement shall be ___ year(s) from ___ to ___ .

  2 Unless either party requests an amendment or termination in writing ___ months before the expiration of the effective period in the preceding paragraph, this agreement shall be extended for the successive period of ___ year(s) and hereafter the same.

【例　文】

第18条　甲また乙は，前条の有効期間中といえども書面による3ケ月の予告をもってこの契約を解除できる。

第19条　乙はこの契約が失効し，または解除された場合には，その失効または解除の日から3ケ月以内に現金をもってこの契約にもとづく既存の債務を弁済しなければならない。

  2　この契約が失効し，または解除された場合においても，その失効または解除のときに存在するこの契約にもとづく個別的契約については，この契約の各条項はその効力を失わない。

第20条　この契約より生じる権利義務に関する訴訟については，第16条を準用する。

【語句の説明】

有効期間中といえども：even during the period of……

3ケ月の予告：notice three months in advance, three month's advance notice

失効し：expire

解除される：terminate

現金をもって：in cash

既存の債務：the obligation which is then still existing, any obligations which are then in existence

失効または解除のときに存在する：existing at the time of such expiration or termination

第 3 章　特約店・代理店契約

この契約の各条項はその効力を失わない：any provisions of this agreement shall still remain effective, shall still survive

準用する：shall apply mutatis mutandis, shall apply with the necessary modification

【訳文 A】

Article 18.　Even during the effective period of this agreement in the preceding article, either KO or OTSU may terminate this agreement by a written notice three months in advance.

Article 19.　In the event that this agreement expires or terminates, OTSU shall pay KO in cash the obligation which is then still existing under the agreement within three months as from the date of expiration or termination.

　2　Even in the event that this agreement expires or is terminated, any provisions of this agreement shall still remain effective for the separate agreement hereunder existing at the time of such expiration or termination.

Article 20.　Article 16 shall apply mutatis mutandis to any litigation involving rights and obligations arisen out of this agreement.

【訳文 B】

Article 17.　Even during the effective period of this agreement as stated in the preceding article, either KO or OTSU may terminate this agreement with three month's advance written notice.

Article 18.　In the event that this agreement terminates or is canceled, OTSU shall pay KO in cash any obligations which are then in existence under this agreement on the date of such termination or cancellation.

　2　Even in the event that this agreement terminates or is canceled, any provisions of this agreement shall still remain effective for any individual sales hereunder existing at the time of termination or cancellation.

Article 19.　Article 15 shall apply mutatis mutandis to any litigation involving rights and obligations arising out of this agreement.

第3節　売買契約

【解　説】
〔訳文B〕では，第19条（訳文Bでは，第18条に相当）第1項の「3ケ月」が削除されていて，3ケ月の予告期間なしに，直ちに現金にて弁済しなければならないので，乙にとってより厳しいものである。

【例　文】

第21条　乙は，甲の請求のある場合にはこの契約または個別的契約より生じたときに，現に存在する金銭債務について，執行認諾文書を付した公正証書の作成手続に異議なく協力する。

第22条　この契約に定めない事項およびこの契約の解釈については別途に協議する。

第23条　甲野乙太郎は連帯保証人となり，この契約およびこの契約に基づく個別的売買に関連して，乙が負担する一切の債務につき乙と連帯してその責を負う。

第24条　（特約条項）

【語句の説明】

甲の請求のある場合には：upon the request of KO
この契約……より生じた：arisen out of this agreement
金銭債務：pecuniary obligation
執行認諾文書：an executory and obligatory wording, a clause of assent to execution
公正証書：notary deed, notarial deed
作成手続きに：in preparing
異議なく協力する：cooperate with ……with no objection
この契約に定めない事項：any matters which are not provided for in this agreement
この契約の解釈：any ambiguity of the interpretation thereof（of this agreement），「疑義」の意味のambiguityをつけ加えている。
別途に協議する：shall be separately settled
連帯保証人：a surety, joint and several
乙と連帯して：jointly and severally together with OTSU
特約条項：matters specially agreed, special agreement

第 3 章 特約店・代理店契約

【訳文A】

Article 21. Upon the request from KO, OTSU shall cooperate with KO, with no objection, in preparing a notary deed containing an executory and obligatory wording for any pecuniary obligation which is arisen out of this agreement or separate agreement and which is then still existing.

Article 22. Any matters which are not provided for in this agreement and any ambiguity of the interpretation thereof shall be separately settled through mutual consultation between KO and OTSU.

Article 23. Otsutaro, Kono shall be a surety, joint and several, and shall be liable for the performance of any obligation, jointly and severally, together with OTSU, which OTSU assumes in connection with this agreement and separate agreements under this agreement.

Article 24. （Matters specially agreed）

【訳文B】

Article 20. Upon KO's request, OTSU shall cooperate with KO, with no objection, in preparing a notarial deed containing a clause of assent to execution of any pecuniary obligation which arises out of this agreement or individual sales and which then still exists.

Article 21. Any matters which are not provided for in this agreement or any ambiguity of the interpretation thereof shall be separately settled through mutual consultation between KO and OTSU.

Article 22. KO agrees to be a surety and shall be liable for the performance of any obligation, jointly and severally, together with OTSU, which OTSU assumes in connection with this agreement and individual sales under this Agreement.

Article 23. （Matters specially agreed）

第3節 売買契約

【例 文】

　上記契約の成立を証するため本書＿＿通を作成し，各署名押印の上，1通ずつを所有する。

　平成＿＿年＿＿月＿＿日

　　　　　　　住所　＿＿＿＿＿＿＿＿＿＿＿＿＿＿
　　　　　　　甲　　　株式会社
　　　　　　　代表取締役　＿＿＿＿＿＿＿＿　㊞

　　　　　　　住所　＿＿＿＿＿＿＿＿＿＿＿＿＿＿
　　　　　　　乙　　　株式会社
　　　　　　　代表取締役　＿＿＿＿＿＿＿＿　㊞

　　　　　　　住所　＿＿＿＿＿＿＿＿＿＿＿＿＿＿
　　　　　　　丙　　　株式会社
　　　　　　　連帯保証人　＿＿＿＿＿＿＿＿　㊞

【語句の説明】

上記契約の成立を証するため：IN WITNESS WHEREOF

本書＿＿通を作成し：this document to be executed in ＿＿；2通ならin duplicate, 連帯保証人がいて3通ならin triplicate.

＿＿年＿＿月＿＿日：日本文の方は，契約書の最初の部分に「年月日」が記載されていないので，最後に「年月日」を記入することになる。しかし，英文の契約書は前文のところに「年月日」がすでに書かれているので，次のような表現になる。
　as of the day and year first above written. また，同じ理由で会社の住所の英訳も省略してある。

各署名押印の上，1通ずつ所有する：execute には，すでに署名し作成する意味が包含されているので，その部分の英訳は省略してある。決まり文句の英訳なので，訳文は一つだけにした。なお，当事者である会社の名称，署名者の氏名，肩書だ

133

第3章　特約店・代理店契約

けにしてある。

【訳　文】

　IN WITNESS WHEREOF the parties hereto have caused this document to be executed in ＿＿ as of the day and year first above written, each party holding one copy.

KO KABUSHIKI KAISHA

―――――――――――――――

President & Representative Director

OTSU

―――――――――――――――

President & Representative Director

―――――――――――――――

Surety

第4章　会社の定款

　近年，外国資本による日本企業との資本提携，吸収合併等が盛んに行われるようになってきた。そうなると当然，定款や決算書等の提示を求められてくる。また，その逆も然りである。この定款には，会社組織，事業目的，株主構成，本店・支店の所在地，決算期等が記載されているため，まず業態を把握するには定款等を調査するのが正確である。ただ，お互いに法律も商習慣も異なる中，正確に翻訳するのも大変な努力を要するだろう。

　そこで，まず最初に米国企業の定款を例に研究してみる。一般的に，米国企業の定款は日本と比べて非常に詳細に書かれており，特に株式の種類，持ち株の記載は顕著である。しかし，ここでは入門書でもあるので，定款翻訳の全体像を掴んでもらうために比較的に日本の定款に近い例文を取りあげることにした。

　この会社は，米国の大企業の100％出資の子会社で株主の構成も簡単であり，その業務内容も親会社の代行のような存在である。ただ，他の米国企業と同様に事業目的は詳細なため一部省略してある。

第4章　会社の定款

第1節　米国会社の定款

【例　文】

Certificate of Incorporation of FAR EAST TRADING, INC.

FIRST　The name of this corporation is FAR EAST TRADING, INC.
SECOND　Its principal office in the State of Delaware is to be located at ＿＿，＿＿ Street, City of Wilmington, County of New Castle, and its resident agent is the corporation, at ＿＿，＿＿ Street, Wilmington, Delaware.

【語句の説明】

certificate of incorporation：英国では memorandum of association を登録すると発行してくれるもの。米国では州務長官に届けると登録官が発行する。また articles of incorporation（定款）と同義語。

FIRST：ここでは「第1条」と訳す。

name：人の場合なら「氏名」とし，この場合は「名称」とする。

be located：～に置く

resident agent：駐在代理人。一般には法律事務所；米国のたいていの大会社がニューヨークやその他の大都市に本社ビルを有しながら税金対策上の理由らしく，その本社の登録上の所在地がデラウェア州ウィルミントン市に置いているが例が多い。

【訳　文】

極東貿易会社の定款

第1条　当会社は極東貿易会社と称する。
第2条　当会社のデラウェアにある主たる事務所を，ニューキャッスル郡ウィルミントン市＿＿＿＿通り＿＿＿＿番地に置き，当会社の駐在代理人をデラウェア州ウィルミントン市＿＿＿＿通り＿＿＿＿番地にある法人とする。

第1節　米国会社の定款

【例　文】

THIRD　The nature of the business and the objects and purposes to be transacted, promoted, and carried on, are to do any or all of the things herein mentioned as fully and to the same extent as natural persons might or could do, and in any part of the world, whether within or without the State of Delaware and whether within or without the United States of America, including specifically, but not by way of limitation, in the Far East, viz.:

　　To conduct promotional, research, developmental and liaison activities on behalf of chemical companies.

　　To purchase, take, own, and hold; to mortgage or otherwise lien; and to lease, sell, exchange, convey, transfer, or in any manner whatever dispose of, real property.

【語句の説明】

the objects and purposes：目的と意図
transact：取り扱う
promote：宣伝する，促進する
carry on：経営する，続ける
Carry out：行う
any of all：一切の，あるいはany and allとすることもある；逆に「一切の」という日本語を英訳する場合には，必ずしもこのようにしないでanyかallのいずれか一つでもよいであろう。
fully：完全に，十分に；full employment＝完全雇用
natural person：自然人；法人ならjudicial person, juridical person
within or without：内外；withoutは「～なしに」ではなく「外の」の意。
by way of limitation：限定として
viz.：すなわち
chemical companies：種々の化学会社
own：所有する
hold：占有する
mortgage：抵当［名］，抵当に入れる［動］

第4章　会社の定款

otherwise lien：もしくは先取特権［名］，もしくは先取特権を設定する［動］；この場合のotherwiseにはあまり強い意味がなく，ただ単に「抵当ではなくて」の「なくて」を暗に意味しているにすぎない。

lease：賃貸する；逆に日本語を英訳する場合には，「賃貸借」なのか「便用貸借」かを慎重に考えて英訳しなければならない。

convey：譲渡する

transfer：移転する

dispose of：〜を処分する

┌─【訳　文】─────────────────────────

第3条　業務の性格およびそれを取り扱い促進し経営する目的と意図は，自然人が為すことができると同じように，完全にかつ同じ程度にデラウェア州の内外を問わず，またアメリカ合衆国の内外を問わず，世界中のいかなる場所においても特に極東を含め，これに限定されずに本定款に定める一切の事項を行うことである。

　　すなわち，諸化学会社に代わって普及，研究，開発および渉外活動を行うこと。不動産を購入し，引き取り，所有し，占有すること；それに抵当権もしくは先取特権を設定すること；それを賃貸し，売渡し，交換し，譲渡し，移転しあるいはなんらかの方法で処分すること。

└────────────────────────────

┌─【例　文】─────────────────────────

FOURTH　The total number of shares of stock which this corporation is authorized to issue is Two Hundred and Forty (240) shares without par value.

FIFTH　The minimum amount of capital with which it will commence business is One Thousand Dollars ($1,000.00).

SIXTH　The name and place of residence of each of the incorporators are as follows:

Name	Residence
＿＿＿＿＿	Wilmington, Delaware
＿＿＿＿＿	Wilmington, Delaware
＿＿＿＿＿	Wilmington, Delaware

└────────────────────────────

第1節　米国会社の定款

【語句の説明】
total number of shares of stock：株式の総数
is authorized to～：～することを許される
shares without par value：無額面株式
minimum amount of capital：資本の最低額
place of residence：たいていの場合は「住所」と訳すが，直訳すると「居住場所」である。
incorporator：会社設立者；会社の定款に署名する者で，会社の発起人とは異なる。
name：このは場合は自然人を指すので「氏名」と訳す。

【訳　文】
第4条　当会社が発行を許される株式の総数は，無額面株式240株とする。
第5条　当会社が業務を開始する資本の最低額は，1,000ドルとする。
第6条　会社設立者それぞれの氏名と住所は，次のとおりである。

氏　　名	住　　所
＿＿＿＿＿	デラウェア州ウィルミントン市
＿＿＿＿＿	デラウェア州ウィルミントン市
＿＿＿＿＿	デラウェア州ウィルミントン市

【例　文】
SEVENTH　This corporation is to have perpetual existence.
EIGHTH　The private property of the stockholders shall not be subject to the payment of corporate debts to any extent whatever.

【語句の説明】
perpetual existence：永久の存在；ここでは「～は存続期間は無期限とする」とした。
stockholder：株主
corporate debt：会社の債務
any extent whatever：程度はどうであれ；ここでは，その程度を問わず。

第4章 会社の定款

【訳　文】
第7条　本会社の存続期間は無期限とする。
第8条　株主の所有財産はその程度を問わず会社の債務の弁済にあてないものとする。

【例　文】
NINTH In furtherance and not in limitation of the powers conferred by the laws of the State of Delaware, the board of directors is expressly authorized:
To make, alter, amend and repeal the by-laws;

　To set apart out of any of the funds of the corporation available for dividends a reserve or reserves for any proper purpose and to alter or abolish any such reserve; to authorize and cause to be executed mortgages and liens upon the property and franchises of this corporation;

　To designate, by resolution passed by a majority of the whole bored, one or more committees, each to consist of two or more directors, which committees, to the extent provided in such resolution or in the by-laws of the corporation, shall have and may exercise any or all of the powers of the board of directors in the management of the business and affairs of this corporation and have power to authorize the seal of this corporation to be affixed to all papers which may require it;

【語句の説明】
in furtherance and not in limitation of〜：〜を拡大するものとして
powers conferred：与えられた権限
board of directors：取締役会
expressly：明示的に，はっきりと；impliedly(黙示的に)の反対語
make, alter, amend and repeal：定め，変更し，修正し，廃止し
by laws：細則，条例
set apart：別に設定し
funds available for dividend：配当に充当可能な
reserve：予備費

第1節　米国会社の定款

alter or abolish：変更し，あるいは廃止し
cause to～：～をさせる
execute mortgage：抵当権を行使する，抵当権を実行する
franchise：特権
designate：定める，指名する
by resolution passed：可決した決議により
by a majority of tho whole board：全会の過半数により；ここではその意味をとり「取締役会全員の週半数により」とした。
one or more committees：一つ以上の委員会，more than one committee なら「二つ以上の委員会」になることに注意。
to the extent provided：定めを限度として
powers of the board of directors：取締役会の権限
the management of the business and affairs：事業および業務の運営
power to authorize～：～させる権限
authorize the seal of this corporation to be affixed to～：～に当会社の社印を押印させる

───【訳　文】───

　　第9条　デラウェア州の法律により与えられた権限を制限するためではなく，それを拡大するものとして，取締役会は次の業務を行うことを特に認められる。

　　　すなわち，細則を定め，変更し，修正し，廃止すること。当会社の配当に充当可能な資金の中から，適正な目的のための予備費を別に設定し，かつそれらの予備費を変更し，あるいは廃止し，当会社の資産および特権に対して抵当権および先取特権を行使することを認め，あるいは認めせしめること。取締役会全員の過半数が可決した決議により，2名以上の取締役よりなる委員会を一つ以上定め，その委員会はそこでの決議もしくは当会社の細則の定めを限度として，当会社の事業および業務の運営に関する取締役会の一切の権限を有し，かつ，その権限を行使することができ，当会社の社印を必要とする一切の書類に，その印を押印させる権限を有するものとする。

第4章　会社の定款

【例　文】

　From time to time to determine whether and to what extent and at what times and places and under what conditions and regulations the books and accounts of this corporation, or any of the mother than the stock ledger, shall be open to the inspection of the stockholders. No stockholder shall have any right to inspect any account or book or document of the corporation, except as conferred by law or authorized by resolution of the directors or of the stockholders.

【語句の説明】

from time to time：時により；sometimes, occasionally とほとんど同義語であるが，法律文書では不思議に from time to time を使う。

determine whether〜：〜かどうかを決定する

to what extent：どの程度まで

at what times and places：いつどこで

under what conditions：どんな条件で

book：帳簿

account：計算書

stock ledger：「株式」と「台帳」となるが，株主名簿を指す；英英辞典には [books kept by a corporation which are entered the names of stockholders and the amount of the holding of each and sometimes other particulars] と説明されている。

be open to the inspection of〜：〜の閲覧のため公開する

except as conferred by law：法律の定めによる場合を除き（別として）

except as authorized by resolution：決議により認められた場合を除き（別として）

【訳　文】

　時により，当会社の帳簿および計算書，あるいは株主名簿以外のものを株主の閲覧のために公開するか否か，公開するとすればどの程度まで，いつどこで，どんな条件と規則でするかを決定し，またいかなる株主も法律の定めによるか，または取縮役会あるいは株主会の決議により認められた場合を除き，当会社の計算書，帳簿あるいは書類を閲覧する権限を有しないものとする。

第1節　米国会社の定款

【例　文】

　To sell, lease or exchange all of its property and assets, including its good will and its corporate franchises, upon such terms and conditions and for such consideration as it sees fit, which may be in whole or in part shares of stock in, and/or other securities of, any other corporation or corporations, when and as authorized by the affirmative vote of the holders of a majority of the stock issued and outstanding having voting power given at a stockholders' meeting duly called for that purpose, or when authorized by the written consent of the holders of a majority of the voting stock issued and outstanding.

　This corporation may in its by-laws confer powers additional to the foregoing upon the directors, in addition to the powers and authorities expressly conferred upon them by law.

【語句の説明】

good will：のれん，営業権
corporate franchise：会社特権
consideration：対価，約因
securities：有価証券
when and as：直訳すると「なので，ときに」となるが，ここでは場合とした；また，「際」に相当する場合もある。if and when が「条件」と「期限」が指することを参照されたい。
affirmative vote：肯定的票決
stock issued and outstanding：既発行および未発行の株式
having voting power：議決権を有する。
meeting duly called：適正に招集された。
the written consent：同意書；日本語の「書」が statement などを使わずに written で表すことのできることに注目。書面なら by document などとせずに in writing と表現できる。
voting stock：議決権つき株式
powers and authorities：直訳すると権力と権限；ここでは単に「権限」とした。

第4章　会社の定款

【訳　文】

　当該目的のために適正に招集された株主会において，与えられた議決権を有する既発行および未発行の株式の過半数の所有者の肯定的票決により認められた場合，あるいは既発行および未発行の議決権つき株式の過半数を有するものの同意書により認められた場合には，その承認に係る条件と対価で，当会社の営業権およびその会社特権を含み，他の会社の株式および，もしくはその他の有価証券の全部または一部の場合もありうる一切の資産および財産を売却し，賃貸し，交換すること。

　当会社は，法により特に与えられた権限のほかに，その細則により上述の権限のほかに追加の権限を取締役に与えることができる。

【例　文】

TENTH　If the by-laws so provide, the stockholders and directors shall have power to hold their meetings, to have an office or offices and to keep the books of this corporation (subject to the provisions of the statute) outside of the State of Delaware at such places as may from time to time be designated by the by-laws or by resolution of the directors.

【語句の説明】

if the by-laws so provide：訳例では，「細則に定めのある場合には」としたが，～so provideは「～会を開催し…を有し，…管理する権限を有するもとする」を指す。

subject to the provisions of the statute：法律の規定にしたがうことを条件として

at such places as may be designated：定められた場所で

【訳　文】

　第10条　細則に定めのある場合には，株主および取締役はときにより細則あるいは取締役の決議により定められたデラウェア州の外で（法律の規定にしたがうことを条件として）会を開催し，事務所を有し，当会社の帳簿を管理する権限を有するものとする。

【例　文】

ELEVENTH　This corporation reserves the right to amend, alter, change or repeal any provision contained in this certificate of incorporation in the manner now or hereafter prescribed by law and all rights conferred on officers, directors and stockholders herein are granted subject to this reservation.

【語句の説明】

reserve the right to～：～する権限を留保する
hereafter：**after this**のことで，将来；「以下に」と混同しないこと。
prescribed by law：法律により定める
subject to this reservation：この(本)留保にしたがうことを条件として；その内容は，「～を改正，修正，変更あるいは廃止する権限を留保する」こと。

【訳　文】

第11条　当会社は，現在もしくは将来において，法律により定められる態様で本定款に定められている規定を改正，修正，変更あるいは廃止する権限を留保し，本定款において役員，取締役および株主に与えられている一切の権限は，本留保にしたがうことを条件として与えられる。

【例　文】

WE, THE UNDERSIGNED　being all of the incorporators, for the purpose of forming a corporation, in pursuance of an Act of the Legislature of the State of Delaware entitled "An Act Providing a General Corporation Law" (approved March 10, 1899) as codified and re enacted as Title 8, Delaware Code of 1953, and the acts amendatory thereof and supplemental thereto, do make and file this certificate of incorporation, hereby declaring and certifying that the facts herein stated are true, and accordingly hereunto have set our respective hands and seals this 5th day of April A. D. 1960.

In the presence of ＿＿＿＿＿＿＿　　　　　＿＿＿＿＿＿＿ (SEAL)

　　　　　　　　　　　　　　　　　　　　＿＿＿＿＿＿＿ (SEAL)

　　　　　　　　　　　　　　　　　　　　＿＿＿＿＿＿＿ (SEAL)

第4章　会社の定款

【語句の説明】

for the purpose of forming a corporation：会社の設立目的のため

in pursuance of〜：〜にしたがって

Act of the Legislature：立法法；すなわち立法に関する法律。このActとLawに、注意しなくてはならないことがある。われわれの考える法律、すなわち同会で可決した法律を指すのがActで、Lawはもっと広い意味で使うことがある。Actは、Act of Congressの省略形と考えられる。だから米国のLawyerから「〜の件に関して日本のCommercial Lawではどうなっているか」と聞かれた場合には、商法の条文だけを調べて答えたのでは正解にならない。その場合には、商法に関連する政令、省令、規則、通達、判例など、すべて研究した上で答えなくてはならない。なお、Commercial Actについて聞かれた場合なら、商法の条文だけ検討して答えればよいから作業は簡単である。

An Act Providing a General Corporation Law：一般法人法を定める法律；日本の「法例」の英訳名を思い起こさせる法律名。法例の英訳はLaw concerning the Application of Laws in General.

codified and re-enacted：法典化され再制定された

Title 8：表題8；米国の成文法はTitle〜と表されている。たとえばTitle 35といえば「特許法」のことである。

acts amendatory thereof and supplemental thereto：acts amendatory of it and supplemental to itのことで、itはAct of the Legislature of the State of Delawareをさす。したがって、「デラウェア州立法法を定める法律の改正・補充法」のことである。

the facts herein stated：ここ（本定款）に記載の事実

hereunto have set our respective hands and seals：それぞれ署名、押印する

A. D. 1960：A. D. はAnno Dominiの略。1960年

in the presence of〜：〜の面前で

【訳　文】

　表題8　1953年のデラウェア法典として法典化され再制定された「一般法人法を定める法」（1899年3月10日、承認）との表題の付されているデラウェア州立法法ならびにその改正・補充法にしたがって、会社の設立目的のため、全員会社設立者であり、下記署名者であるわれわれは、本定

第1節　米国会社の定款

款の証明書を作成，提出し，本定款に記載の事実は真実であることを宣言し，証明し，よって1960年4月5日（公承人氏名〇〇〇〇）の面前でそれぞれ署名押印する。

〇〇〇〇　㊞
〇〇〇〇　㊞
〇〇〇〇　㊞

【例　文】

CERTIFICATE OF ACKNOWLEDGEMENT OF NOTARY PUBLIC

STATE OF DELAWARE)
　　　　　　　　　　) ss.
NEW CASTLE COUNTY)

BE IT REMEMBERED　that on this 5th day of April A.D. 1960, personally appeared before me, the subscriber, a notary public for the State and County aforesaid, all the parties to the foregoing certificate of incorporation, known to me personally to be such, who severally acknowledged the said certificate to be their act and deed respectively, and that the facts therein stated were truly set forth.

　　GIVEN under my hand and seal of office the day and year aforesaid.

　　　　　　　　　　　　　　　　　　　　　———————————
　　　　　　　　　　　　　　　　　　　　　　　(Notary Public)

【語句の説明】

ss.：州務長官；Secretary of State の略

BE IT REMEMBERED：直訳すると「that以下のことを記憶されたい」ということであるが，ここでは「次のことを証明する」とした。

personally appeared：自身で出頭した。

before me：日本の証明書の慣例にしたがい，ここでは「本職の面前に」とした。

subscriber：署名者

第4章 会社の定款

notary public：公証人
aforesaid：上述の
parties to the foregoing certificate of incorporation：上述の定款の当事者
known to me：直訳すると「私に知られている」が，ここでは「自身で認識している」とした。
severally：それぞれ；「連帯して」なら jointly and severally
to be their act and deed：彼らの行為，すなわち自身の行為
the day and year aforesaid：上述の年月日

【訳　文】

公証人の認証証明書

　　　　デラウェア州）
　　　　　州務長官）
　　　ニューキャッスル郡）

次のことを証明する。
　1960年4月5日，全員上述の定款の当事者であることを，本職が自身で認識しているが，上述の州・郡の公証人であり，署名者である本職の面前に自身で出頭し，それぞれ同人らが該支善を作成した旨，ならびに記載された事実が真実である旨，各自認した。
　上述の年月日に，本職の面前でなされた。

　　　　　　　　　　　　　　　　　　　　　○○○○
　　　　　　　　　　　　　　　　　　　　　（公証人）

公証人の認証証明書のサンプルをもう一つ示す。

【例　文】

CERTIFICATE OF ACKNOWLEDGEMENT OF NOTARY PUBLIC

State of California）
　　　　　　　　　）ss.

第1節　米国会社の定款

County of Sacramento）

On this 4th day of September in the year 1991 before me,

　　　　Sadako Otsuno　　　　
（Insert name of notary public）

personally appeared Hanako Kono, personally known to me （or proved to me on the basis of satisfactory evidence） as the person whose name is subscribed to this instrument, and acknowledged that he or she executed it.

NOTARY SEAL

　　　　　　　　　　　　　　　Sadako Otsuno　　　　
　　　　　　　　　　　　　　（Signature of Notary Public）

　　　　　　　　　　　　　　　　　　　　Official Seal
　　　　　　　　　　　　　　　　　　　Sadako Otsuno
　　　　　　　　　　　　　　　Notary public california
　　　　　　　　　　　　　　　　　　Sacramento town
　　　　　　　　　　　　　　My town EXP July 17, 1995

【語句の説明】

certificate of acknowledgement of notary public：公証人の証明書
insert name of notary public：公証人名を挿入
proved to me：本職に対して証明した
satisfactory evidence：十分な証拠；**sufficient evidence** ともいう。
instrument：文書

【訳　文】

　　　　　　　　　公証人の認証証明書

カリフォルニア州）
　　　州務長官）
　サクラメント郡）

第4章　会社の定款

　1991年9月4日，カリフォルニア州の公証人である乙野貞子（公証人名）の面前に，本職がその文書の署名者であることを認識している（あるいは，その旨を十分な証拠により本職に対して証明した）甲野花子が自身で出頭し，本職に対し同人がその文書を作成した旨，自認した。

乙野貞子
（公証人の署名）

㊞

第2節　米国会社の決議書

社名変更に関する取締役会の議事録を例として，会社の決議書に関する英文を解説する。

―【例　文】――――――――――――――――――――――――――

MINUTES OF MEETING OF THE BOARD OF DIRECTORS

A meeting of the Board of Directors of FAR EAST TRADING, INC., was held on the 5th day of December, 1972, at 11 a. m. on the F. B. Building, Wilmington, Delaware.

The following directors were present : A, B, C, being an of the members of the board.

【語句の説明】

minutes：議事録(複数形)

meeting of the board of directors：取締役会

The following directors were present：直訳すると「次の取締役が出席した」となるが，ここでは日本の定款の慣例にしたがい「出席取締役：A, B, C」とした。

―【訳　文】――――――――――――――――――――――――――

取締役会議事録

極東貿易会社の取締役会が，1972年12月5日午前11時にデラウェア州ウィルミントン市F．Bビルにおいて開催された。

出席取締役：A, B, C

―【例　文】――――――――――――――――――――――――――

Mr. A stated that the meeting was called to consider the advisability of amending the corporation's certificate of incorporation to change its corporate name to ABC, Inc., effective January 2, 1973. After discussion of the relevant

151

第4章　会社の定款

factors involved, the directors deemed it advisable to so amend the certificate.

【語句の説明】
was called to～：～するために招集された。
advisability：よいかどうか，すなわち「当否」
corporate name：社名；company name, trade nameともいう。
effective January 2, 1973：1973年1月2日，有効；ここでは「1973年1月2日付で」とした。
relevant factors：関連事項，当該事項
deemed it advisable to～：～することが適正であると考えた
to so amend：直訳すると「そのように改正する，上述のように改正する」こと，すなわち「社名変更」を指す。

【訳　文】
　A氏が，1973年1月2日付で社名をABC社(注：新社名)に変更するための定款の改正の当否を諮るために取締役会が召集される旨述べた。
　当該事項を討議の後，取締役は定款を改正するのが適正であると考えた。

【例　文】
　Accordingly, upon motion duly made, seconded and carried, it was
　RESOLVED, that the Certificate of Incorporation of FAR EAST TRADING INC., be amended, effective January 2, 1973, by changing the Article thereof numbered FIRST" so that, as amended, said Article shall be and read as follows:
　"FIRST The name of this corporation is ABC INC."
and it was
　FURTHER RESOLVED, that the respective managers, of all of the foreign branch offices of the company be, and they hereby are, authorized and directed to carry out all procedures and details necessary to effect such change of name as of January 2, 1973 on all of their bank accounts and other financial and commercial activities, including all pertinent documents and stationery.

第2節　米国会社の決議書

【語句の説明】

motion：動議，申し立て；その動詞は move（申し立てる）。The defense is going to move ～（弁護側は～を申し立てる）。蛇足だが，これを「弁護側はこれから動きだします」と訳した法廷通訳のいたことを記憶している。

motion duly made, seconded, and carried：適式に提出され，賛成され，可決された動議

RESOLVED：決議する

the Article thereof numbered "FIRST"：直訳すると「第1と番号の付されたその条項」であるが，ここでは慣例にしたがい「第1条」とした。

as amended：改正されると，改正された場合；この as amended はここでは特に訳出しなかった。

said Article shall be and read as follows：直訳すると「その条項は～となり，～と読まれる」となるが，ここでは「第1条は次のごとくなる」としてある。

FURTHER RESOLVED：さらに決議する

respective managers：それぞれの(各)支配人，管理職者

foreign branch：外国支店，外国にある支店

managers … be, and they hereby are, authorized and directed to ～：managers … be authorized and directed to ～ と they are hereby authorized and directed to ～ をまとめた文。

authorized and directed to ～：～をなす権限が与えられ，かつ～することを指示される

effect such change：変更する；make such change に同じ。effect（動）～をなす。たとえば effect registration は登録する。

as of January 2, 1973：1973年1月2日現在

bank accounts：銀行口座

financial and commercial activities：経理・営業活動

pertinent documents：関連ある書類

stationery：書簡紙

【訳　文】

　よって適正に動議が提出されて賛成され，可決のうえ，次のごとく決議された。すなわち，極東貿易会社(注：旧社名)の定款は第1条の変更により1973年

153

第4章　会社の定款

1月2日付で改正され，第1条は次のごとくなる。
　「第1条当会社の名称は，ABC社(注：新社名)とする。」
とされ，さらに次のごとく決議する。すなわち，当会社の外国にあるすべての事務所の支配人は，一切の関連ある書類および書簡紙を含め，一切の銀行口座およびその他の経理・営業活動に関して，1973年1月2日現在，その名称を変更するに必要なすべての手続きおよびその他の必要事項をなす権限が与えられ，かつその権限を行使することを指示される。

【例　文】

　Mr. A then stated that as the one stockholder of record of the corporation, he would give the corporation a letter evidencing his consent to the proposed change in name so that a special stockholder's meeting to vote on the amendment would not have to be called. Such consent is to be filed with these minutes.

　There being no further business to come before the board, upon motion, the meeting was adjourned.

————————————
Secretary

【語句の説明】

Mr. A then stated：その上でA氏が述べた

stockholder of record：名簿に記載されている株主

a letter evidencing～：～を証明する書面

proposed change in name：名称変更の提案；inは「おける」ではなく「の」と訳す。たとえば, increase in～は～の増加, decrease in～は～の減少。さらに，英文の形容詞を日本語では名詞に訳すと日本語らしくなることがある。だからproposedを「提案」と名詞形に訳してみた。

vote on～：～について票決する

to be filed with～：～とともに綴じ込む；ここでは「一体となす」と訳した。

there being no further business to come before the board：取締役会において討

第 2 節　米国会社の決議書

議すべき議題がほかにないので
upon motion：申し立ての上
was adjourned：閉会された

【訳　文】

　その上で，A氏はこの改正について票決するための特別株主会を招集する必要のないようにするため，当会社の名簿に記載されている株主の一人として，名称の変更の提案に同意していることを証明する書面を当会社に与える旨述べた。この同意は本議事録と一体をなすものとする。
　取締役会において討議すべき議題がほかにないので申し立ての上閉会した。

〇〇〇〇
秘書

【例　文】

CONSENT

　The undersigned being all of the directors of FAR EAST TRADING, INC. hereby consent to the adoption of the foregoing resolutions.

　Dated: December 5, 1972

――――――――
――――――――
――――――――

【語句の説明】
consent：同意；written consent となっていないが，ここでは「同意書」と訳した。
the undersigned：下記署名者
the adoption of the foregoing resolutions：上述の決議の採択

第4章　会社の定款

【訳　文】

同 意 書

　全員極東貿易会社(注：旧社名)の取締役である下記署名者は，本書により上述の決議の採択に同意する。

　　日付：1972年12月5日

○○○○
○○○○
○○○○

第3節　米国会社の目的の翻訳

前項では，米国会社の定款の目的に関する部分の一部を紹介するにとどめたが，ここでは省略した部分について研究する。

【例　文】

To manufacture, produce, purchase, or otherwise acquire; to hold, own, mortgage, or otherwise lien, pledge, lease, sell, assign, exchange, transfer, or in any manner dispose of; and to trade in and with goods, wares, merchandise, and personal property of any and every class and description; whether now known or hereafter to be discovered or invented.

【語句の説明】

manufacture：製造する
produce：生産する
hold：保有する，占有する
own：所有する
lease：賃貸する
dispose of：処分する
trade in〜：〜を商う，〜を売買する
trade with〜：〜を取り引きする
goods, wares, merchandise：商品；それぞれ少しずつニュアンスの異なる語句なのでカッコの中に原文を挿入することにした。
Personal property：動産，個人的財産
description：銘柄
hereafter：将来；「以下に」を意味するhereinafterと混同しないこと。

【訳　文】

現在知られているか，あるいは将来発見もしくは発明されるかを問わず，あらゆる種類，銘柄の商品(goods, wares, merchandise)および動産を製造，生産，購入あるいは他の方法で取得し；保有，所有，抵当権を設定し，あるいはその他の方法で先取特権を設定，質権を設定し，賃貸，売却，譲渡，交換，移転し，

第4章　会社の定款

あるいはなんらかの方法で処分，売買し取り引きすること。

【例　文】

　　To acquire the goodwill, rights, and property, and to undertake the whole or any part of the assets and liabilities of any person, firm, association, or corporation; to pay for the same in cash, the stock of this company, bonds, or otherwise, to hold or in any manner to dispose of the whole or any part of the property so purchased; to conduct in any lawful manner the whole or any part of any business so acquired; and to exercise all the powers necessary or convenient in and about the conduct and management of such property and business.

【語句の説明】

goodwill：のれん，信用，営業権

undertake：引き受ける

assets and liabilities：資産と負債

firm：会社；これは一応の訳。たとえばlaw firmは「法律事務所」と訳されるが，小規模のものはlaw officeと称せられる。このfirmはcompanyとも異なり，日本の合名会社に近い。

association：組合；これも一応の訳で「社団」とも訳せる。ちなみに財団法人は，foundation.

corporation：法人；これもまた一応の訳。これを場合によっては「会社」と訳す。

in any lawful manner：なんらかの合法的方法で

the conduct and management of property and business：資産の運用および事業の運営

【訳　文】

　　のれん，権利，資産を取得し，人，会社，組合，法人の資産と負債の全部または一部を引受け，それらに対して現金，当会社の株式，債券，その他で支払い，購入したそれら資産の全部または一部を保有し，あるいはなんらかの方法で処分し，取得したそれら事業の全部または一部を合法的方法で運営し，それら資産の運用および当該事業の運営に必要な，あるいは便宜な一切の権限を行使すること。

第3節　米国会社の目的の翻訳

【例　文】

To guarantee, purchase or otherwise acquire, hold, and to sell, assign, transfer, mortgage, pledge or otherwise dispose of, shares of the capital stock, bonds, or other evidences of indebtedness created by other corporations and, while the holder of such stock, to exercise all the rights and privileges of ownership, including the right to vote thereon, to the same extent as a natural person might or could do.

【語句の説明】

assign：譲渡する
transfer：移転する
shares of the capital stock：株式
evidences of indebtedness：債務の証拠
created by other corporations：他の法人が創設した
right to vote on～：～に対して票決する権利，すなわち票決権
a natural person might of could do：自然人が行使しようと思えばできる；あるいは当然に行使できるの意。しかし，ここでは単に「自然人が行使することができる」としてある。

【訳　文】

　株式，債券あるいは他の法人が創設したその他の債務の証拠に対して保証を与え購入し，あるいはその他の方法で取得，保有，売却，譲渡，移転，抵当権および先取特権を設定し，あるいはその他の方法で処分し，それら株式の所有者である期間中，票決権を含め，その所有権に基づく一切の権利および特権を自然人が行使することができると同程度に行使すること。

【例　文】

To employ technicians, experts, and engineers, in every branch of scientific skill and endeavor, and to initiate, direct and supervise their efforts in research, surveys, and investigations, in any and all branches and fields of science and technology and in connection with any matter or thing, enterprise or project conducted and/or to be conducted by or under the supervision of this

第4章 会社の定款

corporation.

【語句の説明】
endeavor：努力
initiate：伝える，起こす
direct and supervise efforts in ～：～に対する努力を指示し監督する
any matter or thing：事物，ものごと
enterprise：事業，企画
project：計画

【訳　文】
　科学技術および企てに関するあらゆる部門の技術者，専門家およびエンジニアを雇用し，かつ科学的技能のあらゆる部門・分野，ならびに当会社の監督により，もしくは監督に基づいて行い／もしくは行うであろう課題，目標，事業，計画に関する彼らの研究，検分，調査に対する努力を伝え，指示し，監督すること。

【例　文】
　To provide a means and method of evaluating, examining, financing, licensing, purchasing, promoting, expediting, developing, testing, producing and marketing in whole or in part all inventions, formulae, machines, scientific instruments, and any other product or service of any and/or every kind and character for the benefit of the shareholders of this corporation for their financial gain and for the benefit of society in general.

【語句の説明】
a means and method：手段および方法
～finance：～に対して融資する
Promote：宣伝普及する
expedite：促進する
market：市場開発する
service：役務

any and/or every：あらゆる，一切の
every kind and character：あらゆる種類および性質の
financial gain：金銭的利益

―【訳　文】――――――――――――――――――――――――――――
　一切の発明，方式，機械，科学的計器，その他あらゆる種類および製品の性質あるいは役務の全部または一部について，当会社の株主の金銭的利益ならびに社会一般の利益のために評価し，試験し，それに対して融資をし，ライセンスを与え購入し，宣伝普及し，促進し，開発し，テストし，製造し，市場開発するための手段および方法を提供すること。
―――――――――――――――――――――――――――――――――

―【例　文】――――――――――――――――――――――――――――
　To register or otherwise obtain any patent or patents for any invention or inventions, or obtain exclusive or other privileges in respect of the same, and to apply for, exercise, use or otherwise deal with or turn to account any patent rights, concessions, monopolies, or other rights or privileges.
―――――――――――――――――――――――――――――――――

【語句の説明】

register or otherwise obtain any patent：特許を登録しあるいはその他の方法で待許を取得し
exclusive：独占的
apply for～：～について申請する
turn to account：活用する
concession：特権；公園とか軍の施設内に売店を出す許可などの特別なもの。
monopoly：独占権

―【訳　文】――――――――――――――――――――――――――――
　発明について特許を登録しあるいはその他の方法で特許を取得し，それら特許に関し独占的あるいはその他の特権（privileges）を取得し，特許権，特権，独占権あるいはその他の権利または特権について申請，行使，利用し，あるいはその他の方法で取扱い，あるいは活用すること。
―――――――――――――――――――――――――――――――――

第4章　会社の定款

【例　文】

To purchase or otherwise acquire letters patent, concessions, licences, inventions, rights, and privileges, subject to royalty or otherwise, and whether exclusive, nonexclusive, or limited, or any part interest in such letters patent, concessions, licences, inventions, rights, and privileges.

【語句の説明】

letters patent：特許証
subject to royalty or otherwise：有償無償を問わず
limited：限定，制限付き
any part interest in～：～の部分的利益

【訳　文】

有償無償を問わず，また，独占，非独占，限定あるいは特許状，特権(concessions)，ライセンス，発明，権利および特権(privileges)の部分的利益かどうかを問わず，特許証，特権(concessions)，ライセンス，発明，権利および特権(privileges)を購入しあるいはその他の方法で取得すること。

【例　文】

To sell, let, or grant, any patent rights, concessions, licences, inventions, rights, or privileges, belonging to the company, or which it may acquire, or any interest in the same.

To enter into, make, and perform, contracts of every kind for any lawful purpose, with any person, firm, association or corporation, town, city, county, body politic, state, territory, government, including any colony or dependency thereof.

【語句の説明】

enter into, make, and perform contracts：契約の交渉をし，締結し，履行する
body politic：国家
territory：準州；ハワイは1959年に州となる前はTerritory of Hawaiiと称せられた。
dependency：保護領

第3節 米国会社の目的の翻訳

【訳　文】

　当会社に属し，あるいは取得できるであろう特許権，特権，ライセンス，発明，権利あるいは特権，あるいはそれらに関する利益を売却，賃貸し，あるいは与えること。

　人，会社，組合，法人，町，市，郡，植民地あるいは保護領を含め国家，州，準州，政府と合法的な目的であらゆる種類の契約の交渉をし，締結し，履行すること。

【例　文】

To borrow money for any of the purposes of the corporation and to draw, make, accept, endorse, discount, execute, issue, sell, pledge or otherwise dispose of promissory notes, drafts, bills of exchange, warrants, bonds, debentures and other negotiable or non-negotiable, transferable or non-transferable instruments and evidences of indebtedness and to secure the payment thereof and the interest thereon by mortgage or pledge, conveyance or assignment in trust of the whole or any part of the property of the corporation at the time owned or thereafter acquired.

【語句の説明】

draw：振り出す
accept：受け入れる，引き受ける
endorse：裏書する
discount：割引きする
promissory note：約束手形
warrants：フラント；地方自治団体から一定額の金銭の支払いを受ける権利を証する書面。
bonds：ボンド，捺印金銭証書
negotiable：流通可能な
transferable：譲渡可能な
instruments：証書，文書
conveyance or assignment：交付または譲渡

163

第 4 章　会社の定款

【訳　文】
　当会社のあらゆる目的のために資金を借りるのは，約束手形，金銭支払指図書，為替手形，ワラント，ボンド，社債およびその他の流通可能あるいは流通不能な，または譲渡可能あるいは譲渡不能の証書および債務の証拠を振り出し，作成し，受け入れ，裏書し，割引し，実行し，発行し，売却し，質入れあるいはその他の方法で処分し，また，所有しているとき，あるいは将来取得した時に当会社の資産の全部または一部に対する抵当権，質権，信託交付または譲渡によりそれ自体ならびにその利子の支払いを確保することである。

【例　文】
　To purchase, hold, sell and transfer the shares of its capital stock.
　To have one or more offices and to conduct any or all of its operations and business and to promote its objects, and to carry on any other business in connection therewith.

【語句の説明】
ono or more officers：一人以上の役員；more than one, 一人を超える，すなわち二人以上と混同しないこと。
Operations and business：運営と業務
Promote its objects：その目的を助長する

【訳　文】
　株式を購入し，保有し，売却し，移転すること。
　一人以上の役員を定め，当会社の一切の運営と業務を執行させ，その目的を助長し，それと関連する他の業務を行わせること。

【例　文】
　To do all and everything necessary, suitable, and proper, for the accomplishment of any of the purposes or the attainment of any of the objects or the furtherance of any of the powers hereinbefore set forth, either alone or in association with other corporations, firms or individuals, andto do every other act or acts, thing or things incidental or appurtenant to or growing out of or

connected with the aforesaid objects or purposes or any part or parts thereof.

【語句の説明】
The accomplishment of…the purposes：…する意図の実現
the attainment of…the objects：目的の達成
the furtherance of…the powers：権限の拡張
the powers hereinbefore set forth：以上述べた権限，上述の権限
either alone of in association with～：単独あるいは～とともに
incidental or appurtenant to～：～にともないあるいは付随して
growing out of～：～から発生する
connected with～：～に関係する

【訳　文】
　単独あるいは他の法人，会社もしくは個人とともに，上述のいずれかの意図の実現あるいは目的の達成，もしくは権限の拡張のために必要，適切かつ適当なすべてのことを行うこと，および上述の意図もしくは目的，あるいはそれらの一部にともない，付随しあるいはそれらから発生し，もしくは関係する一切のその他の行為，物事をすること。

【例　文】
　To do any or all of the things herein set forth as principal, agent, contractor, trustee or otherwise, alone or in company with others.
　The objects and purposes specified herein shall be regarded as independent objects and purposes and, except where otherwise expressed, shall be in no way limited nor restricted by reference to or inference from the terms of any other clause or paragraph of this certificate of incorporation.

【語句の説明】
Principal：本人
agent：代理人
contractor：請負人，契約者
trustee：受託者

第4章　会社の定款

alone of in company with～：単独であるいは～とともに
except where otherwise expressed：別段の記載ある場合は別として
in no way：決して～しない
by reference to～：～に関連させ
inference from～：～から推定して

【訳　文】

　本書に記載された一切の事項を本人，代理人，請負人，受託者としてあるいはその他の方法で単独であるいは他人とともになすこと。

　本書に記載された意図および目的は，独立の目的および意図とみなされ，別段の記載ある場合は別として，本定款の他の条項の条件に関連させ，あるいはそれから推定して，決して制限されたり限定されないものとする。

【例　文】

　The foregoing shall be construed both as objects and powers and the enumeration thereof shall not be held to limit or restrict in any manner the general powers conferred on this corporation by the laws of the State of Delaware.

【語句の説明】
The foregoing：以上の記載
Be construed as～：～と解釈される
The enumeration thereof：the enumeration of it, その例示的記載
be held to～：～とする，～と考える，～と判示する（判決で示す）

【訳　文】

　以上の記載はともに目的および権限と解釈され，その例示的記載はいかなる方法であれ，デラウェア州法により当会社に与えられた一般的権限を制限し，あるいは限定するものではない。

第4節　日本の株式会社の定款

【例　文】

第1章　総　則

（商　号）
第1条　当会社は株式会社後藤商事と称する。

【語句の説明】
当会社：the company, this company
～と称する：shall be called ～

【訳　文】

Chapter 1.　General Provisions

（**Company name**）
Article 1.　The company shall be called "Kabushiki Kaisha GOTO SHOJI."

【例　文】

（目　的）
第2条　当会社は次の事業を営むことを目的とする。
　　1　各種教育を目的とする研修会ならびに学習塾などの企画，開催および運営
　　2　出版物の刊行，企画および販売
　　3　市場調査ならびに宣伝広告業務の企画および開催
　　4　前各号に付帯する一切の業務

【語句の説明】
事業を営む：carry on business, carry out business
～を目的とする：the objects are to ～
各種教育を目的とする：for various educational purposes

第4章　会社の定款

研修会：training courses

学習塾：現在では，Jukuでも理解されるらしい。しかし，定款の中で使えるほどの強力な市民権を得ているとも思われないので，一応 private school とした。

企画：企画することと考えて to plan；開催，運営，刊行も同様に考える。

開催：to hold

運営：to manage

出版物：publication；印刷物なら printed matter

刊行：to publish

市場調査：market research

宣伝広告：publicity and advertisement；しかし，訳例では advertisement だけを使い，宣伝広告業務を advertising business と訳した。

【訳　文】

(**Objects**)

Article 2.　The objects of the company shall be to carry on the following businesses.

1) To plan, hold and manage training courses and private schools for various educational purposes.

2) To plan, publish and sell publications.

3) To plan and conduct market research and advertising business.

4) Any and all businesses incidental to those specified in any of the above items.

【例　文】

（本店の所在地）

第3条　当会社は本店を東京都豊島区に置く。

第4条　当会社の公告は官報に掲載する。

【語句の説明】

公告：public notice

官報：Official Gazette

公告は〜に掲載してする：the public notice shall be given in 〜

第4節　日本の株式会社の定款

【訳文】

(**Location of principal office**)

Article 3.　The principal office of the company shall be located at Toshima-ku, Tokyo-to.

Article 4.　The public notice of the company shall be given in the Official Gazette.

【例文】

第2章　株　　式

(発行する株式の総数および額面株式1株の金額)

第5条　当会社の発行する株式の総数は200株とする。
　　　　当会社の発行する額面株式1株の金額は5万円とする。

(株式の記名式および株券の種類)

第6条　当会社の株式はすべて記名式とし，1株券，5株券，10株券，50株券および100株券の5種類とする。

【語句の説明】

発行する株式：shares to be issued

額面株式：share with par value

株式1株の金額：the amount of each share

株式の記名式：non-bearer share

株券：share certificate

【訳文】

Chapter 2.　Shares

(**Total number of shares to be issued and amount of each share with par value**)

Article 5.　The total number of shares to be issued by the company shall be two hundred (200) shares.

　　The amount of each share with par value shall be fifty thousand yen

169

第4章　会社の定款

（¥50,000）.

(**Non-bearer share and kind of share certificates.**)

Article 6. All shares of the company shall be non-bearer shares and the share certificates be of five kinds, namely, one-share certificates, five-share certificates, ten share certificates, fifty share certificates and one hundred-share certificates.

【例　文】

（株式の譲渡制限）

第7条　当会社の株式を譲渡するには，取締役会の承認を受けなければならない。

（名義書換）

第8条　株式の取得により名義書換を請求するには，当会社所定の書式による講求書に記名押印し，これに次の書面を添えて提出しなければならない。

　1　譲渡による株式取得の場合には株券

　2　譲渡以外の事由による株式の取得の場合には，その取得を証する書面および株券

【語句の説明】

株式を譲渡するには：for transferring a share

取締役会の承認：the approval of the board of directors, あるいはthe approval from the board of directors

株式の取得により：by reason of the acquisition of stock

当会社所定の書式：the application form prescribed by the company

記名押印し：name written and seal-affixed 記名と署名を混同しないこと。

　署名は自身で書いたものだが，記名は他人に書かせたり自分の名前のゴム印を押したりしたもの。著名はsignatureだが記名はsignatureではない。

　「調書には供述者に署名押印させなければならない(shall be caused to **sign** and seal the protocol) 刑事訴訟規則第38条第6項」

　「記名押印しなければならない(……**affix his name** and seal thereto) 刑事訴訟

第4節　日本の株式会社の定款

規則第76条第2項」

次の書面を添えて：together with the following documents

譲渡による：be obtained by way of transfer

譲渡以外の事由による株式の取得：share is obtained for the reason other than the transfer

---

【訳　文】

(**Restriction on transfer**)

Article 7.　Approval shall be obtained from the board of directors for transferring shares of the company.

(**Entry of change of shareholder**)

Article 8.　For making the request for the entry of a change of the shareholder in the registry of shareholders, the application form prescribed by the company shall be name-written and seal affixed together with the following documents.

1) Share certificate, when share is obtained by way of transfer.

2) Document showing the acquisition of share certificate, when share is obtained for the reason other than the transfer.

【例　文】

(質権の登録および信託財産の表示)

第9条　当会社の株式につき質権の登録または信託財産の表示を請求するには，当会社所定の書式による請求書に当事者が記名押印し，これに株券を添えて提出しなければならない。その登録または表示の末消についても同様とする。

【語句の説明】

質権：pledge

信託財産：trust property

株券：share certificate

同様とする：the same shall also apply

第4章　会社の定款

【訳　文】

(**Registration of pledge and indication of trust property**)

Article 9.　For making the request for the registration of a pledge or the indication of trust property regarding the share of the company, the applicant shall affix his name and seal to the application form prescribed by the company and submit the same together with the share certificate attached thereto. The same shall also apply to the cancellation of the registration or the indication.

【例　文】

(株券の再発行)

第10条　株券の分割，併合，汚損等の事由により株券の再発行を請求するには，当会社所定の書式による請求書に記名押印し，これに株券を添えて提出しなければならない。

　　　　株券の喪失によりその再発行を請求するには，当会社所定の書式による請求書に記名押印し，これに除権判決の正本または謄本を添えて提出しなければならない。

【語句の説明】

分割：division

併合：consolidation

汚損：stain

再発行：reissue

再発行を請求する：make the request for the reissue, demand the reissue

株券の喪失により：by reason of the loss of the share certificate；訳例では，株券を share certificate とせずに thereof とした。

除権判決：judgement of exclusion

正本：the original

謄本：certified copy

【訳　文】

(**Reissue of share certificate**)

Article 10.　For making the request for the reissue of a share certificate for the reason of division, consolidation, stain, etc., the applicant shall affix his name and seal to the application form prescribed by the company and submit the same together with the share certificate attached thereto.

For making the request for the reissue of a share certificate by reason of the loss thereof, the application form prescribed by the company shall be noted under the name and seal of the applicant and submitted together with the original or certified copy of the judgement of exclusion.

【例　文】

（手数料）

第11条　前3条に定める請求をする場合には，当会社所定の手数料を支払わなければならない。

【語句の説明】

手数料：charges

前3条に定める請求：request provided for in the preceding three Articles

---

【訳　文】

(**Charges**)

Article 11.　For making the request provided for in the preceding three Articles, the fee prescribed by the company shall be paid.

【例　文】

（株主名簿の閉鎖および基準日）

第12条　当会社は，営業年度末日の翌日から定時株主総会の終結の日まで株主名簿の記載の変更を停止する。

　　　　前項のほか，株主または質権者として権利を行使すべき者を確定するため必要があるときは，あらかじめ公告して一定期間株主名簿の記載の変更を停止し，または基準日を定めることができる。

【語句の説明】

株主名簿：本条ではregistry of shareholderとしてみた。しかし，米国ではstock

第4章　会社の定款

ledgerが一般的らしい。

閉鎖：closure

基準日：record day

営業年度末日：the last day of the business term

〜の翌日：the day after〜；まちがいやすいから注意。長い文章の中にday after December 31とあると12月31日以降などと訳しがちである。この意味は12月31日の翌日以降である。これをthe day after tomorrowが明後日であることから考えると理解しやすい。

終結の日：the day of the termination

前項のほか：文の内容いかんにより，in addition to the provision in the preceding paragraph，あるいはin addition to the preceding paragraph

質権者：pledgee

権利を行使すべき者：the person who exercises the right

確定する：determine

【訳　文】

(**Closure of registry of shareholders and record day**)

Article 12. The company shall suspend alteration of entries in the registry of shareholders from the day after the last day of the business term to the day of the termination of the regular session of the general shareholders' meeting.

　　In addition to the provision in the preceding paragraph, when it is necessary to determine the person who exercises the right as a shareholder or pledgee, the company may give a public notice thereof in advance and suspend alteration of any entry in the register of shareholders for a specified period of time or determine the record day.

【例　文】

（株主の住所等の届出）

第13条　当会社の株主および登録された質権者またはその法定代理人もしくは代表者は，当会社所定の書式によりその氏名，住所および印鑑を当会社に届け出なければならない。届け出事項に変更を生じたときも，その事項につき同様とする。

174

第4節　日本の株式会社の定款

【語句の説明】

届出：notification

法定代理人：agent, proxy, deputy, representative

代表者：representative

印鑑：seal-impression；「印鑑を届ける」とは印鑑そのものを届けるわけではないので，その意味をとって「印影」を表す語に訳す。

届出事項：matters to be notified

【訳　文】

(**Notification of residence, etc., of shareholders**)

Article 13. The shareholder and registered pledgee of the company or the legal representative or agent thereof shall give the company the name, address and seal-impression thereof in the prescribed form of the company. When a change is made in the matter to be notified, the same shall also apply with respect to the matter concerned.

【例　文】

第3章　株主総会

（招　集）

第14条　当会社の定時株主総会は，営業年度末日の翌日から3カ月以内に招集し，臨時株主総会は必要に応じて招集する。

（議　長）

第15条　株主総会の議長は社長がこれに当たる。社長に事故があるときは，あらかじめ取締役会の定める順序により，他の取締役がこれに代わる。

【語句の説明】

株主総会：general meeting of shareholders

必要に応じて：as the occasion demands, when necessary, when it is necessary to do so

〜に事故あるときは：いろいろな訳し方があるが，ここでは in the event of any absence or inability to 〜 とした。

　　あらかじめ定める順序：the order prescribed in advance

第4章　会社の定款

【訳　文】

Chapter 3.　General Meeting of Shareholders

(**Convocation**)

Article 14.　The ordinary general meeting of shareholders of the company shall be convened within three (3) months as from the day after the last day of the business term and an extraordinary general meeting of shareholders shall be held when it is necessary to do so.

(**Chairman**)

Article 15.　The chairman of the general meeting of shareholders shall be the president. In the event of any absence or inability to perform his duty, the other director shall act fort he president by the order prescribed in advance by the board of directors.

【例　文】

(決議の方法)

第16条　株主総会の決議は，法令または定款に別段に定めがある場合のほか，出席した株主の週半数をもって決する。

【語句の説明】

決議の方法：method of resolution

別段の定めがある場合のほか：unless it is otherwise provided

出席した株主：shareholders present

〜の過半数で：a majority of 〜

【訳　文】

(**Method of resolution**)

Article 16.　The resolution of the general meeting of shareholders shall be made by a majority of shareholders present, unless it is otherwise provided by laws or ordinances, or these articles of incorporation.

【例　文】

第4章　取締役，取締役会，代表取締役および監査役

（取締役および監査役の員数）
第17条　当会社の取締役は5名以内とし，監査役は2名以内とする。

【語句の説明】
5名以内：five (5) or less ; less than（未満）とは異なるので注意。

【訳　文】

Chapter 4.　Directors, Board of Directors and Auditors

（**Number of directors and auditors**）

Article 17.　The number of directors of the company shall be five (5) or less and the number of auditors thereof, two (2) or less.

【例　文】

（取締役および監査役の選任の方法）
第18条　当会社の取締役および監査役は，株主総会において議決権のある発行済み株式の総数の3分の1以上に当たる株式を有する株主が出席し，その議決権の過半数の決議によって選任する。
　　　　取締役の選任については累積投票によらない。

【語句の説明】

議決権のある株式：voting stock, voting shares

発行済み株式：issued shares, shares issued

総数の3分の1以上：one-third or more ; more than one-third（3分の1を超える）とは異なるので注意。

議決権の過半数の決議：the (a) resolution of the majority vote

累積投票：cumulative voting

第4章　会社の定款

【訳　文】

(Method of selecting and appointing directors and auditors)

Article 18.　The directors and auditors of the company shall be selected and appointed by a resolution of the majority votes of shareholders present who hold shares representing one-third or more of the total number of voting shares issued.

　　The selection and appointment of a director shall not be made by cumulative voting.

【例　文】

（取締役役監査役の任期）

第19条　取締役および監査役の任期は，就任後2年内の決算期に関する定時株主総会の終結のときまでとする。

　　任期満了前に退任した取締役の補欠として，または増員により選任された取締役の任期は，前任者または他の在任取締役の任期の残存期間と同一とする。任期満了前に退任した監査役の補欠として選任された監査役の任期は，前任者の残存期間と同一とする。

【語句の説明】

任期：term of office

決算期に関する定時株主総会：the ordinary general meeting of shareholders convened in respect of the period for the settlement of accounts

任期満了前：prior to the expiration office's term of office

〜の補欠として：as a substitute for 〜

〜の増員により：due to the increase in the number of 〜

前任者：the predecessor

他の在任取締役：other remaining director (s)

残存期間：remaining period

【訳　文】

(Term of office of directors and auditors)

Article 19.　The term of office of directors and auditors shall be until the termination of the ordinary general meeting of shareholders convened in respect of the period for the settlement of accounts within two (2) years as from his assumption of office.

The term of office of a director selected and appointed as a substitute for a director who retires prior to the expiration of his term of office or due to the increase in the number of directors shall be the same as the remaining period of the predecessor or the other remaining directors.

The term of office of an auditor selected and appointed as a substitute for an

【例　文】

（取締役会の招集および議長）

第20条　取締役会は社長がこれを招集しその議長となる。社長に事故があるときは，あらかじめ取締役会の定める順序により，他の取締役がこれに代わる。

　　　　取締役会の招集通知は，会日の3日前に各取締役に対して発するものとする。ただし，緊急の必要があるときはこの期間を短縮することができる。

【語句の説明】

招集する：convene, call

招集通知：そのまま訳すと「a notice convening a meeting」だが，ここでは，初めに「取締役会を招集するには」という趣旨のことばを使ってきたので，「a notice to that effect（その旨の通知）」とした。

会日：the day set for such meeting

緊急の必要があるとき：in time of emergency

短縮することができる：may be shortened

【訳　文】

(**Convocation of board of directors meeting and chairman**)

Article 20.　The meeting of the board of directors shall be convened by the president who shall be the chairman. In the event of any absence or inability to perform his duty, one of the other directors shall act for the president by the

第4章　会社の定款

> order prescribed in advance by the board of directors.
> 　In convening the meeting of the board of directors, a notice to that effect shall be dispatched to each director three (3) days prior to the day set for such meeting. However, such period may be shortened in time of emergency.

【例　文】
（役付き取締役）
第21条　取締役会の決議をもって取締役の中から社長1名を選任し，必要に応じて副社長，専務取締役，常務取締役各若干名を選任することができる。

【語句の説明】
役付き取締役：Titled directors
取締役の決議：a resolution at the meeting of the board of directors；この場合の「取締役会」は，会合を開くと理解されるのでmeetingを補って訳してある。
必要に応じて：when deemed necessary
専務取締役：senior managing director
常務取締役：ordinary managing director；これらの専務取締役，常務取締役は日本特有の制度なので直訳しておくよりほかに仕方がない。なお，英和辞典の中にはmanaging directorを専務取締役との訳語を掲載しているものもあるが，それでは常務取締役をどのように英訳するのであろうか。もっとも英語にも業務執行担当の役員としてのmanaging directorという語がある。外国法人の日本における登記の際に定款の翻訳をするが，そのときはmanaging directorをケースバイケースで専務取締役と訳したり，常務取締役と訳したりするのが実情である。
若干名：an indefinite or indeterminable number

【訳　文】
(**Titled directors**)
Article 21.　One (1) president shall be selected and appointed from among directors by a resolution at the meeting of the board of directors and an indefinite or indeterminable number of vice-presidents, senior managing directors and ordinary managing directors may be respectively selected and

appointed, when deemed necessary.

【例　文】

（代表取締役）

第22条　社長は当会社を代表し，会社の業務を統轄する。

取締役会の決議をもって，前条の役付き取締役の中から会社を代表する取締役を定めることができる。

（報　酬）

第23条　取締役および監査役の報酬は，それぞれ株主総会の決議をもって定める。

【語句の説明】

当会社を代表し：represent the company

〜を統轄する：preside over 〜

【訳　文】

(**Representative director**)

Article 22.　The president shall represent the company and preside over the business of the company.

　　The director representing the company may be appointed from among titled directors provided for in the preceding Article by a resolution adopted at the meeting of the board of directors.

(**Reward**)

Article 23.　The reward of directors and auditors shall be respectively determined by the resolution of the general meeting of shareholders.

【例　文】

第5章　決　算

（営業年度）

第24条　当会社の営業年度は，毎年9月1日から翌年8月31日までの年1期とする。

第4章　会社の定款

【語句の説明】

年1期：one (1) term per year, single term per year

毎年〜から翌年〜までの年1期とする：one (1) term per year from 〜 every year through 〜 of the following year

---
【訳　文】

Chapter 5.　Account

(**Business term**)

Article 24.　The business term of the company shall be one (1) term per year from the first day of September every year thorough the thirty-first day of August of the following year.

【例　文】

(利益配当)

第25条　利益配当金は，毎営業年度末日現在における株主名簿に記載された株主または質権者に対して支払う。
　　　　配当金がその支払い提供の日から満3年を経過しても受領されないときは，当会社はその支払義務を免れるものとする。

【語句の説明】

利益配当：直訳すると distribution of profits, dividend, profits

毎営業年度末日現在：as of the last day of every business term

3年を経過しても：even if three (3) years have passed, even after a lapse of three (3) years

〜の支払い義務を免れる：be relieved of the obligation to pay 〜

【訳　文】

(**Profits**)

Article 25.　Profits shall be paid to shareholders entered in the register of shareholders or pledgees as of the last day of every business term.

　　When profits are not received even after a lapse of three (3) years as from the day offered for the payment thereof, the company shall be relieved of the

第4節　日本の株式会社の定款

obligation to pay such.

【例　文】

第6章　付　　則

（設立に際して発行する株式）
第26条　当会社の設立に際して発行する株式の総数は額面株式80株とし、その発行価額は1株につき5万円とする。

【語句の説明】
付則：supplementary provisions
設立に際して：at creation, at the time of establishment
額面株式：share with par value
発行価格：issue-price

【訳　文】

Chapter 6. Supplementary Provisions

(Shares to be issued at creation)

Article 26. The total number of shares to be issued at the creation of the company shall be eighty (80) shares with par value and the issue-price shall be fifty thousand yen (￥50,000) per share.

【例　文】

（最初の営業年度）
第27条　当会社の最初の営業年度は、当会社成立の日から平成元年8月31日とする。
（最初の取締役および監査役の任期）
第28条　当会社の最初の取締役および監査役の任期は、就任後1年以内の最終の決算期に関する定時株主総会の終結のときまでとする。

第4章　会社の定款

【語句の説明】

成立の日：the day of coming into existence

【訳　文】

(**First business term**)

Article 27.　The first business term of the company shall be from the date of coming into existence of the company through the thirty-first day of August, 1992.

(**Term of office of first directors and auditors**)

Article 28.　The term of office of the first directors and auditors of the company shall be until the termination of the ordinary general meeting of shareholders convened in respect of the period for the settlement of accounts within one (1) year as from his assumption of office.

【例　文】

(発起人の氏名，住所および引き受け株数)

第29条　発起人の氏名，住所および各発起人が引き受けた株式の数は次のとおりである。

　　　　(住所) _____
　　　　額面株式 _____ 株　　(氏名) _____

　　　　(住所) _____
　　　　額面株式 _____ 株　　(氏名) _____

　　　　(住所) _____
　　　　額面株式 _____ 株　　(氏名) _____

【語句の説明】

引き受けた株式：shares subscribed

第4節　日本の株式会社の定款

> 【訳　文】
>
> (**Name, address and number of shares subscribed**)
>
> **Article 29.** The names, addresses and number of shares subscribed shall be as follow.
>
> (Name)　　(Address)　　(Number of Shares with par-value Subscribed)
>
> _____　_____　_____
>
> _____　_____　_____
>
> _____　_____　_____

　また，英文の定款や契約書の最後に決まり文句として次の文を加える。その意味は，「以上の証として，下記署名者は本定款を作成し，記名押印する。」ということである。

> **IN WITNESS WHEREOF,** the undersigned have caused these articles of incorporation to be executed, affixing their names and seals thereto.

第5章　法務関係における米国の教育

　相当以前から日本では，米国大学院のビジネススクールでMBA（Master of business administration）の取得について頻繁に話題になり，MBAを取得することがビジネス界のエリートコースにのるパスポートであると言われてきた。ところが最近では，米国で法律を教えている機関としてlaw schoolについて話題になるようになり，その機関の名称をカタカナでロースクールと表現したり，法律大学院などとも称せられている。わが国でも社会の実態に即した，法律の実務教育が始まろうとしている。
　また，米国ではロースクールの他に，あまり知られていないようだがpublic administrationを教授する官庁職員向けの高等教育機関がある。この教育機関は，ビスネス界におけるbusiness administrationと同程度の教育機関として重要視されている。
　筆者が日本で学校教育を受けた時代の大学教育の目的は，「学問のための学問を研鑽すること」とか，「深遠な真理の探求をすること」とかを主眼としていたようである。そして，いわゆる世俗の実利的技能を教えることは，専門学校等の職能訓練学校で教えることであり，大学の教育はもっと高い理想を求めているのだと言われてきた。
　このような教育を受けてきた筆者は，米国のスクール（大学院レベル）へ留学した時に大変戸惑った経験がある。それは，米国のスクールでの授教内容は実社会で即役立つようなカリキュラムが多く，非常に実利的なものであった。このことは，ロースクールはむろんのこと，その他のスクールでも同様であった。
　それから比べると時代も変わり，現在では日本の大学生の数も筆者の時代の約40倍にもふくれあがって200万人とのことであるのだが，依然として実利的でなく，直接職業に技能に結びつくものではない。またそのような教育に不安を感ずる学生も相当数おり，彼等は大学に通うと同時に専門学校に通い職業技能を身につけようとしているとのことである。そこでいわゆる「ダブル通学」という言葉も生まれている。米国流の教育ならこんな無駄な「ダブル通学」は必要がないのではないかと考える。
　本章では，公務員志望者や官庁相手に許認可を求めるビズネスマンに役立つ学問（いわゆる，官庁作文の勉強）を授けるpublic administration関係のコースのさわりを紹介する。

第5章 法務関係における米国の教育

第1節　Public Administration関係のスクール
― 官庁関係の文章作成 ―

　筆者が通学したスクールの外国人留学生は，student advisor（学生の相談係）の許可がなければ希望する学科目を聴講することができない仕組みになっていた。そのstudent advisorは学部長がを兼任していた。その学部長にforeign affairs 101を聴講するように強く勧められ，school of foreign affairsのコースを取る機会が与えられた。その学部長は，「これが本学で教えるすべての講義の中で最高の講義である」と述べ，さらに「その講義は，自分が教えるから」と，そっと付け加えた。そこで，教授の意に添うのがベストと考えてforeign affairs 101を聴講することにしたわけである。

　そこで，講義の資料の一部を使用し，その雰囲気を紹介することにする。この資料から，演習の目的が官庁作文の勉強であり，公務員として上司のために「提言書」を作成する要領を会得させることを意図してしていることが理解できる。

　このように米国のpublic administration関係の演習は実利的なものである。

　以下に，foreign affairs 101のカリキュラムの一部を適当に分解し，説明の都合上しかるべき見出しをつけ，その内容を紹介する。

　なお，各自が割り当てられた課題の作業にはいる前に，教授は要領よく重要な専門用語について説明している。

① Objectives derive from national interests, but they are conditioned by the need to come to terms with the national interests of other states. In consequence of this interplay, objectives come to designate the particular kinds of adjustment sought, ……．

　　（目的は国益に由来するが，ただし，他国の国益と調整する必要性に条件付けられる。この相互作用の結果，目的は特殊の〜を定めることになる。）

② Policies are a specific courses of action designed to achieve objectives.

　　（政策は，目的を達成するために定められた特定の行動方針である。）

③ Commitments denote specific undertaking in support of policy.

　　（コミットメントは政策を支える明確な約束を示すことである。）

④ To summarize: the national interest is what a national feels to be essential to its security and well-being; objectives are concrete interpretation of the national

第 1 節　Public Administration 関係のスクール

interest spelt out as precise guides to action in the light of a current pattern of international relations; policies are thought-out courses of action for achieving objectives; and commitments are specific undertakings in support of a given policy.

（要約すると，国家の利益は国家がその安全で健康な生活をおくるための必須なことであると考えるものであり，目的は国際関係の現行パターンに照らし，行動の正確な指針として明白に定められた国益の具体的な解釈であり，政策は目的を達成するために考えられた方針であり，コミットメントは与えられた政策を支える明確な約束を示すものである。）

a）演習趣旨

【例　文】

The assignment for these two weeks will be the preparation and discussion of a series of "position papers." For the purpose of the exercise, assume that a regional conference of U.S. Chiefs of Mission with their senior economic advisors, together with senior U.S. military commanders in the area has been called to meet in Istanbul on March 25. This conference will discuss problems of the area, with a view to assessing the success of present U.S. policies and recommending such changes and shifts of emphasis as seem to be necessary. Your task is to prepare a "position paper" for the use of the Assistant Secretary of State during these discussions.

【解　説】

国際関係の演習課題は，現実に動いている今日の話題（カレント・トピック：current topics）である。そのためは，学生たちは課題が面白くて堪らないらしく，生き生きとしてデスカッションに参加していた。居眠りをするような学生は一人もいない。

【語句の説明】

the assignment：課題
the preparation and discussion：作成と討議
a series of：一連の
position paper：提言書；「a detailed report that recommend a course of action on a

第5章 法務関係における米国の教育

particular issue」と言うことで，提言書に相当するようである。
for the purpose of the exercise：演習目的のため
assume that〜：〜とする
a regional conference：地域会議
U.S. Chiefs of Mission：米国使節団の長たち
their senior economic advisors：上席経済顧問団
senior U.S. military commanders：上席米軍指令官団
has been called to meet：開催するべく招集された
with a view to〜：〜の目的で
assessing the success of present U.S. policies：米国の現政策の成功の見込みを評価する
recommending：勧告する
changes and shifts of emphasis：重点の変更および移行
for the use of the Assistant Secretary of State：国務副長官の使用のために

【訳　文】

　この2週間の研究課題は，一連の「提言書」の作成とその提言書について討議することである。演習目的のため，上席経済顧問団と米国使節団長たちの地域会議が，その地域にある上席米軍指令官団とともに，3月25日にイスタンブールにおいて開催されるべく招集された。この会議は，米国の現政策の成功の見込みを評価し，必要と思われる重点政策の変更および移行を勧告する目的で，その地域の問題を討議することである。皆さんの課題は，この討議中に国務副長官の使用に供すべき「提言書」を作成することである。題目は以下の通り。

b）課　題

【例　文】

　Subjects are as follows:
　"The Position of the U.S. with respect to
　　　1. Turkey
　　　2. Iran
　　　3. Pakistan

> 4. Israel
> 5. Claims of Greece toward Cyprus
> 6. Egypt
> 7. Libya
> 8. Regional arrangements in the Middle East
> 9. Navigation of the Turkish Straits
> 10. The defense of the Middle East
> 11. The Arab-Jewish Conflict."

【解 説】
　学生に与えられる課題は，等しく「米国の立場」であるが，各人の課題内容は異なる。そのため，関連事項の対象も学生数にあわせて11項目ある。各人が割り当てられた事項について提言書を作成する。しかし，それらの課題の討議には全員が参加し情報を共有する。このようにして，分担業務と共同業務の両方の訓練を受けるので，結果的にクラス全員が全部の課題に参加することになる。ただし，その提言を報告する学生は，クラスメート達の猛烈な批判，反論にさらされることとなる。また，この討議を通じて各人のレポートの出来映えもクラス全員に開示され，採点の透明性は確保されている。

　このようなトレーニングを通じて，実社会に出る前から実際的な業務の扱いを覚えるわけである。したがって，官庁や企業に勤めようが，入社時からスタッフの一人として戸惑うことなく仕事に就けることになる。

【語句の説明】
Subjects are as follows：題目は以下の通り
the Position of the U.S. with respect to～：米国の立場，ただし～について
regional arrangements in the Middle East：中東における地域的取り決め
the Arab-Jewish Conflict：アラブーユダヤ紛争

─【訳　文】─────────────────
　題目は以下の通り。
　　米国の立場，ただし以下の事項について，
　　　1. トルコ
　　　2. イラン

第5章　法務関係における米国の教育

3. パキスタン
4. イスラエル
5. キプロスに対するギリシャの主張
6. エジプト
7. リビア
8. 中東における地域的取り決め
9. トルコ海峡の航行
10. 中東の防衛
11. アラブ－ユダヤ紛争"

c) 作成要領

【例　文】

Prepare "position papers" in the following format.

Facts Bearing on the Problem

Here include a brief history of pertinent events leading up to the present situation, a brief description of the present situation, and why this situation is of importance to the U.S.

U.S. Objectives

To include a statement of U.S. objectives toward the country, as you see them, and a brief discussion of possible alternatives.

Policy Formulation

A statement of what U.S. policy is (if you can find it); what you think our future policy (courses of action) should be. Include your reasoning for selection of these courses from among alternatives.

All members of the class should read Bookings, Major Problems of U.S. Foreign Policy, p 266-282.

第1節　Public Administration関係のスクール

【解　説】
　ここでは，提言書の書き方について教示している。すなわち，「関連事実」，「アメリカ合衆国の目的」「政策の策定」の構成方法である。日本では，古来から漢詩の構成に由来する「起，承，転，結」によって文章を構成しなさいなどと教えられてきた。しかし，この方式が何時でも当てはまるわけではない。米国のスクールでは，このように具体的な文の構成方法も教えている。筆者はサラリーマンになってから，このような教育法の恩恵を随分受けている。

【語句の説明】
facts bearing on the problem：問題に関係する事実
a brief history of pertinent events：関連性のある出来事の簡単な由来
leading up to the present situation：現在の情勢に至るまでの
a brief description of the present situation：現状の簡単な記載
is of importance to the U.S.：米国にとって重要な
a statement of U.S. objectives：米合衆国の目的の記載
toward the country：当該国に対する
as you see them：皆さんが見たように；皆さんの理解するところにしたがい
a brief discussion：簡単な論考
possible alternatives：可能な代替え案
policy formulation：施策の策定
what U.S. policy is：合衆国の政策の現状；米合衆国の政策はどのようなものであるか
if you can find it：見い出すことができれば
what our future policy should be：わが国の将来の政策はどうあるべきか
your reasoning：理由付け
for selection of these courses：これらの方針を選択するについての
all members of the class should read～：クラスの全員は～を読むこと

【訳　文】
　"提言書"は，以下の形式で作成すること。

　問題に関係する事実
　現在の情勢に至るまでの関連性のある出来事の簡単な由来，現状の簡単な記

第5章 法務関係における米国の教育

載および,なぜこの情勢が米国にとって重要であるかということを本項に挿入すること。

合衆国の目的

皆さんの理解するところにしたがい,当該国に対する合衆国の目的の記載と可能な代替え案に関する簡単な論考を挿入すること。

政策の策定

合衆国の政策はどのようなものであるか(見い出すことができれば);わが国の将来の政策(たどるべき道筋)はどうあるべきかについて記載すること。複数の代替え案の中から,これらの方針を選択する理由付けを挿入すること。

クラスの全員は,次の書物を読むこと。

Brooking発行,合衆国の対外政策の主要問題,266-282頁

d)作成準備で注意すること

【例　文】

Note: Emphasis will necessarily vary considerably in treatment of the different topics. Where policy seems well crystallized and non-controversial, as in the case of Turkey and Libya, a historical review will constitute the major effort of the paper. Be alert, however, to detect emergent issues. Refer to Congressional hearings (particularly "lead off" statements by Cabinet officers) and Committee Reports, in connection with U.S. assistance program. Overlap of subjects is intentional; papers should be prepared independently, although there is no objection to exchange of information on sources.

【解　説】

実に実践的な教示である。このような訓練が,後に社会に出てから仕事の上で筆者にとって大いに役に立った。この時の提言書作成の準備段階における資料探しでは,教示されている国会議事録や種々の政府関係委員会の報告のほかに,News WeekやTimeなどの週刊誌,Washington Post, New York Times, Wall Street Journalなどの新聞等々,図書館で入手可能な限りの文献を読みあさったものだった。

この準備段階では,お互いに労力を惜しむことなく教室外でも徹底的に協力し合

第 1 節　Public Administration 関係のスクール

う。しかし，一旦教室でレポートの発表段階になると，打って変わって厳しい雰囲気となり，「昨日の友は，今日の敵」となり，報告者に対して激しい議論を交わし，実に活気のある討議が展開された。

【語句の説明】

emphasis will necessarily vary considerably：重点が，かなり違ってくることは当然であろう

treatment of the different topics：異なるトピックのとり取り扱い

well crystallized and non-controversial：充分に煮詰まっていて議論の余地のない

a historical review：歴史的検討

constitute the major effort of the paper：提言書作成の主たる努力の対象を構成する

be alert：警戒せよ

to detect emergent issues：表面に現れようとしている問題を探知するべく

refer to～：～を参照せよ

Congressional hearings：国会公聴会

"lead off" statements by Cabinet officers："リード　オブ"声明文；閣僚による"口火を切る"声明文

overlap of subjects：課題の重複

intentional：意図的

independently：独立して；演習の内容によっては共同作業のこともある。

no objection to～：～に対して異議がない

exchange of information on sources：資料(情報)源の交換

──【訳　文】──────────────────────────

注意：重点が取り扱うトピックの相違によりかなり違ってくることは当然である。政策が充分に煮詰まっていて議論の余地のない場合には，例えばトルコやリビアの場合のごとく，歴史的検討が提言書作成の主要な努力の対象となるであろう。しかし，表面に現れようとしている問題を探知するべく警戒すること。合衆国の援助プログラムに関して，国会における公聴会の議事録(特に閣僚による"リードオフ"声明文)および委員会報告を参照すること。

　　課題の重複は意図的にされている。提言書は独立して作成すべきであるが，資料源を交換することは差し仕えない。

第5章　法務関係における米国の教育

> 第2節　speechとdramaの英語訓練
> ── 日本人ビジネスマンにも参考になる ──

　米国におけるスクールをもうひとつ紹介する。それは，本来は米国人相手に「英語の教育・訓練」をするもので，日本では大学ではなく，俳優学校や演劇学校などの専門学校で行うものであろう。

　その後，student advisorに気に入れられたせいか，聴講生の形でschool of speech and dramaのコースにも参加することが許された。ただ，credit（単位）をもらえるわけではないし，専攻学科の授業を欠席することは許されなかった。それでも大変楽しいコースであった。時によっては，現役のactor, actress, comedianがボランティアで非常勤講師を務めることもあった。

　このコースの教育は，英語を頭で勉強して理解することではなく，あくまでも体（口）を使って英語を身につける訓練である。例えば，日本の中学校の英語教育の初期段階で，"the" の発音について，母音の前では「ði」，子音の前では「ðə」と発音することを教えるはずである。しかも，教師が数分説明するだけである。ところが，米国のschool of speech and dramaスクール（大学院並）では，その発音の訓練を厳しく行う。そこで，筆者の手元にある資料の一部を利用して，その訓練状況を再現してみる。

a）教材1（theの発音）

WEAK FORM OF THE DEFINITE ARTICLE

ði　before consonants
ðə　before vowels

the dust	the ox	the ocean	the address
the view	the arm	the owner	the advance
the guess	the aim	the apple	the opinion
the court	the oil	the order	the attempt

第2節　speech と drama の英語訓練

the brook	the ice	the equal	the account
the use	the owl	the uncle	the American
the union	the hour	the evening	the operation

DRILL: The offer, the music, the honor, the tongue, the organ, the nation, the arch, the year, the horse, the air, the increase, the wind, the afternoon, the island, the iron, the object, the one, the outside, the young, the egg, the hair, the interest, the inch, the article, the army, the over, the art, the age, the book, the house.

at the end	to the house	in the air
at the back	up the stairs	on the arm
to the front	in the evening	by the hour
in the middle	in the morning	on the floor
from the beginning	in the afternoon	in the article

in the exercise	to the old	on the ice
than the eye	in the open	by the Indian
in the ocean	by the inch	of the English
to the uncle	than the offer	in the interest
at the office	from the officer	to the advantage

the opinion of the student	the subject of the talk
to the east of the house	at the edge of the forest
the age of the patient	at the end of the book
the aim of the lesson	the rent by the year
the advice of the minister	the walk across the fields

the style of the artist	the sound of the alarm
the length of the answer	the songs of the Americans
the center of the earth	at the appearance of the ghost
the heat of the iron	the property of the army
the house on the island	the answer to the question

第5章　法務関係における米国の教育

その訓練に出席する学生は約10名。授業は，教官が次々と指名して学生に読ませる。読ませてみて，教官の意に添わない発音をすると遠慮なくその発音を矯正し，何回か繰り返して発音させ，満足する発音ができると「その発音を10回繰り返したら，着席してよろしい。」となる。そして，その学生が終わって着席すると同時に，次の学生を指名して同じことを繰り返す。したがって，10名のクラスの中で常に3名くらいの学生が発音練習をしているという，恐ろしく緊張させられる訓練である。

ネイティブだからといって，常に満足するような発音ができるわけではない。彼等も例外でなく，発音を繰り返し矯正される。その学生達も誰一人文句も言わず，発音の癖(方言)を直すために真っ赤な顔をして矯正・練習している。

このような方法で訓練した日本人がいるので紹介しよう。その人とは，昭和20年代に一世を風靡したNHKの英会話講師「カムカムおじさん」こと，平川唯一氏である。同氏は，ワシントン大学のschool of speech and dramaの出身とのことである。

筆者もこのコースの匂いを嗅ぐ程度だが，それでも外資企業の会議のおける発表などでは，さほど苦労するようなことはなかった。

また，終戦後のことだが，日本語を上手に話すアメリカ兵にあうことがよくあった。彼等の一人に聞いてみると，ミシガン大学で日本語を半年勉強しただけだとのことだが，聞いて吃驚したものだった。彼は，おそらく上述のようなスクールで，日本語について集中訓練を受けたのではないかと思われる。

このように，熱心にして優れたネイティブの先生がいれば，やり方によっては，日本でも能率的な英会話教育ができるのではないだろうか。

b) 教材2　(tの発音)

日本語の発音はすべて母音で終わるので，日本人は英語の子音で終わる語の発音は苦手である。だから「t」の音も彼等のように歯切れ良く発音できない。教官はこのことに気づいたらしい。「君はt音の発音がよくない。」と言われ，特に筆者のために以下の表を準備してくれ，繰り返し練習するよう指導してくれた。参考までに紹介する。

第2節　speech と drama の英語訓練

t^h

ten to ten	better times
time to talk	entertain Thomas
touch a toad	not an adult
take a taxi	it is not
tame a tiger	wrote a letter
till tomorrow	told a story
taught a tot	stole a stone
not a bit	stay for tea
tan or white	stare at Anne
wrote a story	stamp a letter
greatest effort	stop a taxi
take some tea	store a table
bought a steak	toast and tea
determine to tell	teach him better
want a towel	determine to tell
hint of winter	thought of Esther
tender steak	a mighty effort
later date	to hate a tyrant
bitter taste	humiliating mistake
went at eight	a salty taste
ate a steak	after ten tomorrow
start a motor	put it away
point at Alice	vast as a city
didn't attempt it	dressed in tatters
tell them about it	hating to fight

第5章　法務関係における米国の教育

```
British subject            senator from Texas
to the tent                quoted his daughter
suffocating heat           itemized list
plenty of time             wouldn't eat it
pointed retort             critical moment
```

　そのほか，「l」と「r」の発音が良くないと，rather（どちらかといえば）とlather（石鹸の泡）を繰り返し練習させられたのは，懐かしい思い出である。ところで，中国語は英語の文法に似ているので，中国人は一般的に英語になじみ易いく実際に堪能な人が多いのだが，「l」と「r」の発音になると，彼等は「r音」の発音が苦手なようだ。注意しているつもりでも，rice（米）をlice（シラミ）と言ってしまうことが多いと聞く。

c）教材3（英文のリズム）

　英会話では，たとえ発音が悪く流暢でなくとも，リズム（語調）が的確ならば会話はスムーズに行くものである。言葉のリズムに慣れ，そのリズムに乗って話せるようにすることが大切である。実際に，終戦後の連合国（主に米軍）占領下で軍関係で働いていた人の中で，小学校もまともに出ていない人たちでも，英語で仕事をこなせる人がたくさんいた。彼らは，教室で文法や単語を学習していたわけでなく，会話の中から発音のリズムを覚えていったのであった。

　筆者も最近次のような経験をした。これはリズムの重要性を改めて納得させるものである。

　それは，パソコンによる英語音声入力のため，ソフトに筆者の音声を慣れさせるための学習訓練をしたときである。

　先ず，英文音声入力用ソフトの音声認識能力を高めるために，最初に「Kyoto」と相当丁寧に読み込もうとしたところ，その反応は「Kyodo」だったり，「Shoko」となってしまう。ところが，「I went to Kyoto」と一応のリズムを持ったセンテンスなら完全に聞き取ってくれる。そこで気をよくして，次に学習資料として英字新聞の記事を使ったが，新聞記事の中の日本の地名や氏名など，ソフトにとってなじみの薄い固有名詞が出てくるため，文脈を把握するのが難しいらしく，英文のリズムが自然でないようである。そのせいか，筆者による口述を正しく認識することがで

第2節 speechとdramaの英語訓練

きなかった。そこで，筆者がサラリーマン時代にネーティブの人達から受け取ったプライベートなレターやメモを資料として使用してみたところ，口述を容易に捕捉し，優れた認識能力を示した。このように，会話のような手紙やメモなどで使われている極めて自然な話し言葉だと，認識能力が高まるようだ。

そのような英文のリズムに慣れさせるようにする資料が，ここで示す教材3である。この教材は英文のリズムのほんの一部を紹介するものであるが，その構成を以下に示す。

① 単独の「æ」の発音
② 二つのストレスからなる語群
③ ストレスのある語の発音は「æ」，ストレスのない語の発音は「i」
④ 「æ」と「e」および「e」と「æ」からなる語句
⑤ 「æ」と「ɛ」からなる語群および「ɛ」と「æ」からなる語群

		æ		
I	cat	fact	plan	land
	fact	fat	bag	sad
		Strong forms of-		
	am	an	and	as
	at	can	had	has
	have	shall	than	that

II TWO-STRESS GROUPS

Carry it back.	They began to act.
Her hat is black.	The band is practicing.
He ran rapidly.	They planned their actions.
She thanked the man.	We handed him the apple.
They sat on the sand.	The animals gathered.
He carried the bag.	Perhaps he can catch it.
The battle began.	They were happy to have them.

第5章　法務関係における米国の教育

They travel led to the valley.	We understand its value.
He has bad manners.	We will stand at the back.
He is gland he is a caption.	They are in that bank.

III　These words have æ in the stressed syllables, i in the unstressed syllables.

began	rapid	captain	carry
family	happy	practice	valley

IV

æ and e

to hand him the letter	That's what he says.
to thank him pleasantly	They were glad to settle it.
planning to separate them	She hasn't read it.
to have had his breakfast	The man was dead.
understanding the question	We were glad to send it.

e and æ

his best hat	The weather was bad.
any land	She felt sad.
anything he has	He's the head of the family.
in every act	We'll attend to the matter.
attending to the matter	They sat on the bed.

V　　　　　TWO-STRESS GROUPS

æ and ɛ

to command the animal	on the narrow path
a bad master	perhaps he would rather
to carry the plants	ran past

第 2 節　speech と drama の英語訓練

happened to ask	sat on the grass
the happy dancers	stand fast

ɛ　and　æ

after the battle	commanding them to stand on it
half the facts	a chance to practice it
a branch of the family	to ask for apples
to laugh at the man	an answer he can understand
the last act	to dance with the captain

著者略歴　後藤 浩司（ごとう ひろし）

昭和27年 3月　北海道大学法学部卒業（旧制）
昭和29年 7月　渡米，ニューヨーク州バード大学にて準備教育をうける
昭和29年 9月　「フルブライト計画」に基づき，ヴァージニア大学大学院に入学，国際関係論（John Gange教授）と共に，米国憲法（James Hart教授）専攻

〔職　歴〕
昭和25年 8月―同26年 3月　札幌北海学園高等部にて英語講師
昭和30年10月―同39年12月　米空軍法務部，法律顧問（Attomey Advisor）
昭和39年12月―同63年 7月　米国会社 ローム アンド ハースアジア，法務・特許本部長（日本，韓国，台湾，香港，中国担当）
昭和42年 3月―平成 3年 4月　東京有機化学工業株式会社，特許顧問
昭和49年 4，5月：特許庁の要請により，欧米（WIPO，西独特許庁，フランス特許庁，英特許庁，米国特許庁）商標制度調査団に団員として随行
　現在，国際渉外事務を専門とする行政書士業務のかたわら，東京都並びに米国ライオグランデ大学日本校にて講師を務める
　日本工業所有権法学会，日本国際経済法学会，東京都行政書士会（新宿支部），日米協会各会員

主な著書
米国特許法の理論と実務，A.I.P.P.I.日本部会
工業英作文，冨山房
技術英訳の発想法（技術には法技術を含む），ビジネス・オーム
技術英文の作法（技術には法技術を含む），ビジネス・オーム
特許ライセンス英語表現辞典（専門用語の解説と共に，工業所有権関係の英文作
　　　　成のための参考辞典），ビジネス・オーム
キリストの健康法，共著（第2章 訳者の言葉，第3章 エッセネ派の平和福音書
　　　　（翻訳），第6章(1)，太極拳と私），中国仙道健康研究会
法務英語入門（増補Ⅱ版），信山社
原文で読む「米国憲法入門」，信山社

法務英語入門―改訂第Ⅱ版

2001年（平成13年）　2月25日発行

著　者　　後藤浩司
発行者　　今井 貴・四戸孝治
発行所　　信山社サイテック
　　　　　〒113-0033　東京都文京区本郷6－2－10
　　　　　TEL 03-3818-1084　FAX 03-3811-8530
発売所　　㈱大学図書
　　　　　TEL 03-3295-6861　FAX 03-3219-5158
印刷／製本　松澤印刷／渋谷文泉閣

Ⓒ後藤浩司　2001　Printed in Japan　ISBN 4-7972-2621-8 C3382

著者　後藤浩司

会社法務英語入門

Ⅰ．定款・登記編／増補版

Ⅱ．人事／雇用編（1），（2），（3）

Ⅲ．対外交渉・契約編（1），（2）

体裁：Ａ５判　全編1,172ページ　　全編セット　本体：16,000円（税別）

【関連図書のご案内】

簡明　法務英語［英和／和英］用語集　　本体：2,500円
原文で読む［米国憲法入門］　　　　　　本体：2,000円